Corporate Entertaining as a
Marketing Tool

Also by Andrew Crofts and published by Mercury Books

Using Television and Video in Business

Corporate Entertaining as a Marketing Tool

Andrew Crofts

MERCURY

First published in 1992
by Mercury Books
Gold Arrow Publications Limited
862 Garratt Lane, London SW17 0NB

Typeset in Palatino by Phoenix Photosetting, Chatham, Kent
Printed and bound in the United States of America by
Bookcrafters, Chelsea, Michigan

British Library Cataloguing in Publication Data is available

ISBN 1–85251–161–3

Contents

Introduction

All over the world business people are coming to realise the importance of corporate entertaining, because they are learning to appreciate the importance of human relationships within the business context. Different nations, however, are reaching these conclusions from different starting points.

In America there is a long history of providing imaginative incentives for staff. Successful US companies have known for years that people need to be motivated in order to perform well, and they have used corporate entertainment as one of the ways of doing this. While some of Britain's most successful companies acknowledge the truth of this fact, few of them get beyond setting up schemes for their sales forces.

On the other hand, because of the glories of their social calendar the British recognised the power of corporate entertainment as a marketing tool aimed directly at the customer, or potential customer, some time ago, while the Americans are only just starting to experiment with this concept.

The Japanese are closer to the British in their appreciation of the power of customer entertainment, although they are also historically skilled at building staff loyalty on a scale unheard of in both America and Europe.

Whether you are using corporate entertainment within the company or outside in the marketplace, the results are the same. You will see improved performance on the

1

'bottom line', and this will make the concept of interest to all types of managers, particularly those in sales and marketing departments.

In both situations – inside and outside the company – you are dealing with *people* and *relationships*, developing them in order to enhance the financial success of your company. In this book I will be looking at the right and the wrong ways of trying to do this, and demonstrating just how powerful corporate entertainment can be as a marketing tool. It is no exaggeration to say that it is possibly the single most powerful ingredient in the marketing mix for some companies.

To research the market I have talked to people who both buy and sell corporate entertainment, and particularly to those who are crusading for the industry to be more widely recognised as a force in the marketing mix. As a result of my research I am thoroughly convinced by their arguments that, first, corporate entertainment is a marketing tool of massive potential, and, second, very few companies are yet harnessing that power effectively.

What I have set out to do here is to explain why it will work, and I then go on to give advice on how to make it work successfully for you. Because of what has happened in the past, many people in the business world are afraid of using corporate entertainment in case others accuse them of extravagance and self-indulgence. This fear is completely unfounded. It is like saying that something which tastes nice cannot possibly be good for you. In reality not only should corporate entertainment be a pleasure for all involved; it should also be entirely justifiable as a business practice.

The message of this book, therefore, is that corporate entertainment works – as long as you do it right!

Chapter 1

What Is Corporate Entertainment?

'Corporate entertainment is about providing a reward for someone, or creating an opportunity to make, enhance or correct an impression about your company, service or product. It is about creating an image and remaining in the memory or your target audience.'

David Tonnison, managing director
of the Marketing Organisation

Corporate entertainment is a precision marketing tool, probably the most precise currently available. It can be directed at one person or at several thousands. The degree of success achieved depends upon the skill, ingenuity and hard work of the people operating it.

It is about forging and strengthening relationships with people who are important to the success of your business. Those people could be customers or employees, potential customers or members of the press, members of the local community or governmental law-makers. Whoever they are, you need to get to know them better; more importantly, you need them to get to know you better.

Corporate entertainment covers a wide range of different activities, the majority of which can have a dramatic and direct impact on the success of a marketing campaign, and consequently on the financial health of a company. To be a success, however, these activities must be an integral part of marketing campaigns, planned and budgeted for from the beginning to ensure that they hit their targets precisely, with devastating effect and with no wastage.

3

Corporate entertainment encompasses any event that is organised by a company to entertain other people when the company has an ulterior motive beyond the wish simply to provide their guests with a pleasant experience. The activities can be divided into two main categories: external and internal.

External Activities

Selling to Existing Customers

This involves using entertainment to persuade your existing clients to spend time with you, so that you can work to increase their loyalty and meanwhile find out more about them as people, and about their needs and problems.

Talking to Potential Customers

This involves using entertainment to tempt potential customers to come and meet you, so that you can give them the best possible impressions of you, as well as specific selling messages.

Talking to Other Parties

This involves using entertainment to reach other influential groups that companies need to talk to, such as politicians, the press or the local community around a factory. They can all be reached and influenced through the skilful use of corporate entertaining.

Internal Activities

A Motivation Event

This could be a prize at the end of a lengthy motivational scheme, such as a trip to Europe on Concorde, a day at the races or a cruise round the Caribbean. It could also be a gala dinner, either at the end of or during a motivation scheme, at which guests can be informed of what is happening, and inspired to compete in a way that will be profitable for the company.

A Conference Event

A certain amount of entertainment content might be needed in a business conference, whether to lighten the atmosphere, to provide a distraction or to help with team-building and educational tasks.

A Familiarisation Trip

This could mean taking a team from one factory or office to visit another within the same group, so that people can meet and see how other parts of the company operate. It could also be a trip round a supplier's or a customer's premises to improve understanding of the buying or selling cycle. And it could involve taking people – customers, the press or financial analysts, for example – to see a product or service in action.

A Family Day

An increasing number of companies are introducing the concept of a family fun day, sometimes to celebrate the opening of new premises and sometimes simply as a 'thank you' or morale booster. It might take the form of a small, local fête or, in a larger company, could mean the setting up of a complete funfair.

A Staff Celebration

This could be a standard Christmas staff party or an event to celebrate the winning of a big order. It could be an intimate dinner in an exotic location or a huge themed ball.

The History of Corporate Entertaining

The entertaining of customers, potential customers and employees is as old as trade itself. The business lunch in the best restaurant in town, the conference held in Monte Carlo or Hawaii – these are concepts with which everyone is familiar, and which these days have a rather old-fashioned ring to them. Most successful business people now drink very little and eat lightly during the day; they will need to see a sound business reason before accepting an invitation that will take them away from their desks or their families. Most are also well travelled, and therefore not particularly excited by the idea of another trip – unless it is cleverly packaged to woo them. Before accepting an invitation they need to see that they will achieve something as a result, and they also need to be tempted by something out of the ordinary before they can be persuaded to attend a social event.

At the same time, host companies have become more conscious of the bottom line. Expense accounts are more closely scrutinised these days than might have been the case in the past, and the analysis of business relationships has become a science as well as an art.

Companies now study carefully how they win new business through personal contact, just as in the past they analysed how to motivate their staff to stay with them and achieve better results, or how to create more effective direct-marketing campaigns. They now know what they want to achieve through their business relationships, and consequently they can set out with definite plans of how to succeed.

In the same way, motivational and incentive entertaining to boost the performance of sales teams has been with us for several decades, and has grown in sophistication until it is now accepted as part of any marketing and sales strategy. In the most forward thinking of companies, incentives are used equally for all, from production staff to the frontline people who actually deal with customers. Entertainment is a major part of virtually any motivational campaign, and many companies have gone on from there to recognise the benefits of planning and organising entertainment with a specific goal in mind. They have now turned to other areas of sales and marketing, to see how entertainment skills might be exploited to maximum advantage.

Instead of simply inviting a customer out to lunch and pouring as much drink as possible down their throat, or taking a group off to the races for the day with a vague idea that they will increase their orders from their hosts as a result, the more far-sighted companies are now planning their corporate entertainment with the same amount of care as they give to their advertising and direct-mail campaigns.

Britain is among the world's most sophisticated countries in the corporate hospitality industry, and that sophistication has largely grown out of the summer social season.

Most of the big social events – the ones closely associated with the Royal Family, for instance – take place during the two or three months of high summer. They include events such as Wimbledon, Royal Ascot and Henley. Once so exclusive, and still deemed so by many people, they used to provide an ideal vehicle for corporate entertainers to impress people. As with a box at the opera, lavish private arrangements at any of these events attracted the sorts of people who would never have been interested in accepting an ordinary lunch invitation.

Despite the fact that everyone has since jumped on the bandwagon, corporate entertainment organisers have found ways of ensuring that these occasions still work, by improving the experiences they have on offer and upgrading the packages. However, the cutting edge of the British corporate entertainment industry has moved on, scaling much more sophisticated heights in the products, packages and advice that they can offer. The favourite buzz-phrase at the moment is 'tailor-made products'. This compares favourably with the often despised 'off-the-shelf products' that have become so popular and have consequently lost some of their original glamour.

If it works to take someone to a famous horse race in their own country, how much more effective it would be to take them next year to one in a foreign country. If this year your customers learned how to shoot clay pigeons, maybe next year they would like to shoot real game on the estate of some stately home, with the lord of the manor at their side advising them on style. Perhaps they would like to go wine-tasting at the world's best vineyards, attend a grand prix or a superbowl, go to Disney World or the carnival in Rio, stay on a private island in the South Pacific or take a fishing trip in the Arctic, play polo with the Prince of Wales or dine at the White House.

As Philippa Bovey, who runs Advantage Hospitality from Washington and PJ Promotions from London, says:

> The British and Americans have completely different styles for the entertainment of customers. In the US everyone is far more relaxed. For many American companies corporate entertainment of clients means buying 100 tickets to a golf tournament and handing four to a client, telling him to bring his wife and kids along and come to the company's 'tent'. The tent will be an unlined, unfloored canopy, and they will be serving iced Coke, hamburgers and hot dogs. If they are sponsoring an event, an American company is likely to have thought through the implications of the media coverage in great detail before buying, but will not have seen any particular marketing value to be gained from hospitality. In Britain the exact opposite might hold true.

British customers of corporate entertainment expect to receive five-star treatment, to be made to feel special and to sample life-styles they would not have access to on their own.

By far the biggest player in the British corporate entertainment industry is Keith Prowse Hospitality. Managing director Peter Selby explains:

The industry in Britain really started when the Open Golf Championship allowed some caterers to put up a tent at the beginning of the 1970s. The other major events soon saw that this was a way of generating valuable revenue, which would mean they could stay out of the clutches of sponsors, which meant they could retain control of their events. Until then the long business lunch was the main method of business entertaining, but that was already waning as people found that they just didn't have the time for big meals in the middle of every working day.

It was in the mid-1970s that Expotel, the hotel reservations agency, started Supersports in order to actively help market hotel bedroom bookings instead of just processing them. A few years later they bought Keith Prowse, the country's oldest and best-known ticket agency, creating Keith Prowse Hospitality. As Peter Selby says:

> We started by selling the packages for incentive purposes, but our clients told us that they wanted to use them for entertaining their customers as well. We suddenly realised that we had discovered a new industry. Agents then started springing up everywhere, buying hospitality and reselling it. Some of them were real pirates who failed to deliver what they promised, giving the industry a lot of bad publicity. That is the situation which now has to be remedied.

Although the industry started by taking people to sports events, it has now broadened out to include the arts. Peter Selby again:

> The arts are good because people are looking for something different, and the arts people are looking for ways to make money. We approached Stoll Moss theatres, for instance, and suggested that they refurbish the royal retiring rooms in their theatres, which were very seldom used, and we now market them as part of overall packages, generating food and champagne sales for the theatres and giving our clients a wider choice of events. It also means that we can provide some events all year round, whereas most sports are strictly seasonal.
>
>   You can use any sort of event for entertainment purposes if

people want to go to it. It could be an agricultural show, or it could be a trade fashion show. As long as the target market is interested in the subject, it will work.

The scope of the corporate entertainment industry is as wide and as deep as the world itself. While people have dreams and ambitions, there will be opportunities for others to make them come true, and to forge profitable relationships in the process.

'Corporate entertainment is a classic below-the-line skill,' says Eddie Hoare, managing director of Elegant Days, 'alongside sales promotion and public relations. Until now, however, it has been seriously underrated.'

Where It Fits in the Marketing Mix

David Tonnison of the Marketing Organisation explains:

Marketing is about creating a process that moves people through from a position where they don't know anything about you to their knowing who you are, liking and trusting you, purchasing from you and then continuing to purchase from you.

Initially the targets have to be the companies which might buy from you, not the individuals who sign the orders or the cheques, because there may be other people within those companies whom you have to influence first. These are all the people who advise the ultimate customers who sign the orders. They are the ones who make recommendations, and they are the people who will eventually work with whatever product it is you are selling and whose opinions will be sought and valued.

It may be that you never actually get to meet the person within a company who is your actual customer, but you can still get them to buy by educating and influencing the people around and below them.

You start by identifying the companies you want to do business with, then you find a person connected to the buying process, name them and qualify their involvement.

Once you have taken the first steps, you then have to keep going, building as accurate an overall picture as possible on the totality of people who will influence the buying decision you want taken. How are they connected? What are their different responsibilities? We actually draw up diagrams showing how our starting person (who might be quite minor in the final analysis) interrelates with everyone else.

This diagram will have as much information as possible about all the individuals involved, and once we know enough, we can start to decide how to use marketing to create the right understanding of us, our services and products within the target company.

We will focus on different people within that target company, more or less frequently, depending on their influence on the buying decision and the stage they have reached in their understanding of us as a supplier. We would seldom start the relationship with an invitation to a corporate entertainment event, at least not at a high level. A target would already have received other communications from us in the form of direct mail, public relations, advertising, seminars and presentations in their office, or they might have heard about us because their assistants talk to our sales people before they actually received any sort of invitation to an entertainment.

The initial contact through corporate entertainment should come when we know that there is a strong possibility that they could become customers. It could take the form of a lunch meeting, a game of golf, or a full-blown motivational campaign ending with a trip to Barbados – whatever is suitable for the individual and the situation.

The events that are sold in the corporate entertainment business are just the commodity – the hardware, if you like. The software is the marketing skills that decide who you are going to target, why and what with. While it is crucial to get the commodity right, that is not the hardest part. A lot of corporate entertainment is executed sloppily in a marketing sense, although the events themselves may run perfectly well.

According to Philippa Bovey:

In many cases, corporate entertainment could be far more relevant to a company than advertising. If you are a specialised

11

construction or engineering company, for instance, you will know who your potential customers are. There may be only a few dozen of them in the whole world. It would therefore be completely inappropriate to advertise in the mass media in the way that fast-moving consumer-goods manufacturers do.

Likewise, professionals such as bankers, insurance agents, accountants and solicitors will succeed or fail on the relationships they manage to build with their client bases, not on the number of new inquiries they manage to generate. It is possible that an advertisement could be a starting point in their marketing campaign, but it would be corporate entertainment that reaped the real rewards.

Customer Care

Most companies of any size now have some sort of customer care programme installed. One of the main aims of that programme will be to generate customer loyalty and to pull customers up the 'loyalty ladder', graduating from being one-off purchasers to becoming occasional buyers, then moving on to being regulars and finally advocates, spreading the word about how good your company is and bringing new business to your door at no extra cost to you.

Suppose for a moment that you could take everyone from the bottom of the ladder in your business and lift them to the top; – imagine what a dramatic effect that would have on your profits. The only way you can do it is by adding value to the product or service you are offering, and the only way you can do that is by forming relationships with the customers so that you can discover what their needs are, explain why you do things the way you do, hear their complaints, and show them that you are the best person for them to do business with.

In his book *Customer Care Management* (Heinemann Professional Publishing), author and trainer Andrew Brown lists the reasons why a company might need to instigate a customer care programme:

- To maximise customer retention.
- To create or increase brand loyalty.
- To minimise price sensitivity.
- To create a perceived difference in a similar 'commodity' style market.
- To achieve a maximum number of advocates who will sell on for the company.
- To create a reputation for being a caring, customer-oriented company.
- To maximise any edge you have over the competition.

All these goals can be achieved by using corporate entertainment as part of the customer care mix. Entertaining people will not be the only thing you do, but it will certainly be a powerful tool in the right hands.

Brown urges his readers to be 'customer friendly'. Taking the phrase at its most literal, what can be more friendly than inviting people to an event to help you get to know them better?

Who Pays

On the whole the budgets for corporate entertainment tend to come from sales or marketing departments. Ideally, they should be included in a marketing budget right from the start, but often they are tacked on at the end if there is any spare money.

It is hard to quantify exactly how much money is spent on corporate entertainment. Do you count all the business lunches with potential and existing customers, for instance? Do you count the staff Christmas party? Do you count the entertainment side of the sales conference? Do you count the incentive scheme that took your sales people away to a Caribbean island, or the sales promotion scheme that gave the winners a romantic weekend away in New Orleans? Do you count the money you spent on sponsoring your favourite sporting event?

In an ideal world perhaps all these things should be put together and assessed for their relative value. If, for instance, you are spending several thousand pounds a year on business lunches that are organised in a haphazard and spontaneous manner, it might be better to channel that money into a planned entertainment programme for the same people, the same number of times, but giving them something more memorable than a three-course lunch in an expensive local restaurant, and at the same time ensuring that the marketing objectives are being met in a planned and controlled way as a consequence.

Every penny spent on building relationships and goodwill within your business is a legitimate business expense, and should be included in the budget just as formally as the money that is going into an advertising or direct-marketing campaign.

Chapter Summary

- Corporate entertainment is about:
  creating and improving relationships;
  creating the right impressions;
  rectifying any inaccurate impressions;
  exchanging information;
  making contacts;
  building loyalty;
  motivating;
  selling.
- It can be aimed at internal audiences through motivation schemes, or at external audiences as part of sales and marketing strategies.
- It involves everything from a simple meal to a full-scale holiday, from visits to spectator events in the sports and arts worlds to participative events of every sort.
- It is a precision marketing tool.
- It should be at the pinnacle of the marketing mix.
- The events themselves are just the hardware; the software is the marketing skills that surround the events.
- A corporate entertainment policy can be an integral part of a customer care programme.
- Corporate entertainment activities within a company need to be identified in all their shades, and budgeted for professionally.

Chapter 2

Why Do It?

'The only selling effort that is deemed more effective than corporate hospitality is the use of a direct sales force.' This was the conclusion reached in 1990 in an objective, independent analysis of the corporate hospitality industry, carried out by Business Marketing Services Ltd (BMSL) and called *The Effectiveness of Corporate Hospitality*.

It is a powerful claim, coming as it does from the mouths of people who have actually tried corporate entertaining and have measured the results against alternative marketing methods like advertising, sales promotion and direct mail. The reasons that corporate entertainment was considered so effective by the companies using it were:

- It was so precise and so controllable.
- It involved no wastage (being particularly suitable for reaching the top 20 per cent of customers, who provide companies with 80 per cent of their business), as long as it was done well and targeted accurately.
- It provided an ideal selling atmosphere.
- It provided the chance of partner involvement, which 'no other type of business-to-business selling and marketing can achieve'.
- It allowed them to measure its effectiveness by monitoring sales and margin performance achieved with the customers who were entertained.
- It could play a major role in differentiating companies from their competitors.

- It provided long-term memorability, whereas 'other marketing efforts do not normally achieve such a lasting impact'.

BMSL concluded: 'Corporate hospitality is seen as more effective and better value for money than advertising, brochures, exhibitions and direct mail in influencing exisiting customers.' In many of the companies surveyed, they claimed,

> a closely linked combination of salesforce and corporate hospitality would be the best way to sell to existing customers. Marketing spend should be concentrated on these two activities, relegating the importance of advertising, exhibitions, direct mail, etc. to a secondary level.
>
> Using a highly motivated sales team and well-researched and planned corporate hospitality would be the best way to achieve maximum returns from limited budgets.

Despite this fulsome praise for the concept, the report goes on to suggest that few of the people who use corporate hospitality do so as effectively as they could.

'What many host companies fail to realise,' they concluded, 'is that an investment in researching the target audience can significantly improve the returns from the event.' This is a view shared by all the many professionals now working to make the industry more accepted as the potentially powerful marketing tool that it is.

'Eighty per cent of corporate hosts are not clear about why they are doing it,' says Simon Morris of the Profile Partnership. 'They just think it sounds like a good idea and they've got the budget to do something. What they haven't got is a clear brief.'

This means that 80 per cent of them are missing an opportunity to undertake some highly targeted precision marketing.

The Power of Precision Marketing

First, it is important to understand what is meant by precision marketing, so that we can see just where corporate entertainment fits into the picture.

Precision marketing means finding out exactly who your most likely customers are, and then targeting all your sales efforts and expenditure on to those people, ignoring the millions of others who might buy from you but equally well might not.

Suppose for a moment that you have a finite budget with which you could afford to do two things (the choice of options would almost certainly be wider, but we will narrow it down for the sake of argument). You could either buy a full-page advertisement in a publication that reaches several million people or organise a day in which you meet with 100 of your most important potential customers, get to know them and let them get to know you and your products.

If you choose to go with the advertisement and then a month after it has appeared you realise that it has made no difference to your level of inquiries or sales, what are you going to do next? You will just have to chalk it up to experience and try something different.

If, on the other hand, you succeed in getting 100 prospects to the right place at the right time, you will have 100 strong potential leads to follow up in any way you think fit, and you will also have gained a great deal of vital market information that you can use to take you forward.

Let's take another example. You have decided to take a stand at a major industry exhibition. This means that a great many of your staff will be tied up for several weeks, preparing for the event and then looking after the stand, and you will have to pay a great deal for the construction of the stand itself. You know how much it is going to cost you and you know who you want to reach (again, assume that there are 100 key people). Suppose for a moment that you take that budget and direct it more precisely at that target market. There are various alternatives.

If you choose the exhibition, you will have a highly uncomfortable few days on the stand waiting for your targets to arrive. They may turn up at just the right moment, but then again, they may come when you are engaged in talking to someone else, and move off before you have had time to speak to them. Worst of all, they may wander past your stand without seeing you, or not bother to come to the exhibition at all. At best you have managed only to get a few minutes of their time standing or sitting in an uncomfortable location (it doesn't matter how many sofas you put on a stand, or how well made the coffee is, you are still in the middle of a noisy exhibition hall and nobody is truly relaxed in such circumstances; there are always other people coming and going and background noise). It is certain that they are talking to at least a dozen of your competitors in the same day, so the chances of their remembering you with any particular clarity are greatly reduced.

If, however, you choose to put the money towards corporate entertainment you can approach the same people directly, set up a day that they will thoroughly enjoy and during which you are bound to be able to talk business for at least as long as you could on an exhibition stand, and probably much longer. You will be in pleasant, relaxed surroundings of your choice, finding out all about one another. They are going to go away with a greater knowledge of your company and a feeling that you are genuinely pleased to be able to work with them.

Alternatively, you could mix the two by using corporate entertainment to get the right people to an exhibition stand at the right time. Suppose you are launching a new product at a major industrial show. You could have an 'A' list of your most important targets, and invite them to the stand on a specific day to see your product and then have lunch with you. You could then have a longer 'B' list of people who you could invite to a drinks reception to see the product at another time, sending them invitations that will get them into the show free (this will work particularly well if it is a show they will be coming to anyway, and will otherwise have to pay for).

The entertaining could then be done on the stand if you have the space and catering arrangements, or in one of the private suites provided by most of the major exhibition venues. By using corporate entertainment in this way you will be able to exert more control over what happens during those few days, who you get to spend time with and what information is exchanged.

Part of a Long-term Campaign

In fact you will never be presented with such a stark choice, because in order to get those 100 names and coax them along to the event, you will probably need to incorporate the entertainment into a wider advertising or direct-marketing campaign. You are not going to be able to write to your 100 best potential customers cold and expect them to turn up when you ask them. You will have to target them carefully, find out about them, let them know about your company and build enough of a relationship for them to be willing and keen to accept your invitation. You may well have to use other marketing means, such as advertising and exhibitions, in order to trawl for the prospects that are worth pursuing and entertaining.

You will also need to plan how you are going to follow up on any interest that may be shown at the event. It would be heartbreaking to have 100 potential clients keen to buy and nothing ready to sell to them, or no infrastructure strong enough to serve them all efficiently.

The corporate entertainment you organise, therefore, will be just one link in any direct-marketing campaign, but it may well be the second most important link after the sale itself.

Works for Everyone

It will be relatively easy to see who your major prospects are if you are selling aircraft parts worth many millions, or machine tools that can be of use only to a finite number of manufacturers. Other companies, you might argue, need to advertise their wares using a scatter-gun approach rather than the single rifle shot. It is undoubtedly true that most public consumers, for instance, cannot be isolated and identified if you are trying to sell them breakfast cereals or furniture polish. However, the fact that you cannot reach the end consumer with corporate entertainment does not mean you cannot aim for other people further up the selling chain.

In order to reach a consumer of fast-moving consumer goods effectively, for instance, you need to gain maximum shelf space in the best retailing outlets. The people with whom you should therefore be building relationships are the retailers, the people who make the decisions about which product is displayed prominently, which is given most point-of-sale support, and which is stocked in the greatest quantities. These people need to be informed about just how you are going to promote your product to the public and about its selling points. They will also need to know that you are a company worth doing business with, one that will make sure they don't run out of stock and deal efficiently with any customer complaints. All these messages can be conveyed through the medium of entertainment.

Your Best Prospects

Your best prospects for new sales are always going to be found within your existing customer base, the people who already know you and your products. Having achieved the most difficult part, which is making the first sale, you have established a relationship, however tenuous, and this can now be built upon.

In many companies the old cliché that '80 per cent of business comes from 20 per cent of the customers' is startlingly true. It is therefore critical that those 20 per cent receive better treatment from you than from anyone else. If you ignore them while chasing after new business, you are never going to build a solid base from which to grow.

In order to improve your relationship with these people, you need to spend time getting to know them. This is vital for a number of reasons:

- You want to know what it is they need and want that you could be giving them.
- You want to be in a position to explain to them, if it is necessary, why your prices are going up.
- You want to make them feel personal loyalty towards you.
- You want to be able to find out if they have any complaints so that you can rectify matters.
- You want them to know just how much you value their custom.
- You want them to talk about you in glowing terms to other people.

Because they are already your customers, you have far greater access to information about them and you can therefore plan corporate entertainment to fit their tastes exactly.

The best way to win new customers is by word of mouth, which means that you have to build a reputation with your existing customers and impress them so much that they recommend you, your products and services to other people.

Standing out from the Competition

As standards in most industries rise all the time, and technology makes products more uniform, the only way for many companies to differentiate themselves from the competition is in the field of service and personal relationships.

All other considerations being equal, customers will often decide to buy from one supplier rather than another simply because they like the people involved and feel comfortable with them. If the products of two rival companies are identical, why buy from someone whom you don't completely trust, or with whom you are not going to enjoy dealing?

Given that this is often the case, anything you can do to strengthen your personal relationships with customers, and make them like you more, is going to help make you stand out from the competition. The stronger your relationship is, the harder it is going to be for any competitor to muscle in and steal your clients.

A Tool for Your Direct Salesforce

In a perfect world a direct salesforce is still the ideal way for most companies to achieve sales. However, as we are not living in a perfect world, there are a few drawbacks:

- Good sales people are hard to find.
- Good sale people cost a lot of money.
- Keeping people on the road costs a lot more money.

There are very few really good sales people around and very few companies can now afford to keep large direct salesforces in action. This explains why so many are turning to database marketing, telephone marketing and all the other options that are so much cheaper.

If you do have sales people, however, a programme of

corporate entertainment events will be a powerful selling tool for them.

- It will provide them with a reason to get to know their customers better (in order to pick the right event to suit their tastes).
- It will give them something to talk to the customers about.
- It will give them an opportunity to spend more time with those customers on a social basis in a relaxed atmosphere where no one is on their guard.

Why Do It for Employees?

Companies are coming to realise that, after their customers, their own people are their greatest asset. Anyone can invest in machinery and all the other inanimate ingredients of a business, but only the best companies can get the best people to join them, and then keep them. Those employees will go on to help make the best companies even better, thus widening the gap between them and the competition.

To win and keep the best people, companies need to concentrate on building and maintaining good personal relationships.

Let's assume that you have a limited sum of money in a budget that is dedicated to improving sales. You could use it either to hire a new sales person for a year or to take your existing team off somewhere, get to know them and their problems, and find ways to motivate them into increasing their performance by 10 per cent.

Given that your new recruit might or might not work out, and will certainly take a few months if not more to start getting results, the chances are that you would be well advised, for a better return on your investment, to opt for motivating your existing people. Even if it just helps by cutting down staff turnover, or improves the company's image in the recruitment marketplace, your investment will have been amply repaid.

Existing employees, like existing customers, are important corporate assets. They are already part of your culture, have probably undergone expensive training and were probably not cheap to recruit. The successful management of human resources has, quite rightly, become one of the major subjects of debate in the business world in recent years. The fundamental truth here, though, as in all human relationships, remains the same: if you treat people right, they will be loyal and hard-working. By 'treating people right', I mean:

- communicating with them:
- letting them know how much you value them:
- doing all in your power to help them lead enjoyable and rewarding working lives.

Corporate entertainment achieves all of these. It isn't just a question of heaping rewards on to the highest-achieving sales people; it is about treating everyone well, giving them reasons to feel warm about the company they are working for and using corporate entertainment as a medium for effective communication.

You might use corporate entertainment to say 'please' or 'thank you' or 'well done'; to demonstrate your product or service to a relevant audience; to celebrate an achievement; or simply to get to know someone better.

The golden rule that should be emerging from this chapter is that, whatever form of corporate entertainment you opt for *you must have a reason*. It should never simply be an indulgence or a habit ('we always do it that way'). Each event must be an integral part of a larger plan.

David Tonnison has an example of the wrong approach:

> I have a client who likes to go skiing in Europe. So every year he takes his sales team on a trip. It costs him around £40,000 and most of them hate it. None of them can afford the extras, like

the price of a beer. But he will not be dissuaded from repeating the exercise every year. That is not using corporate entertainment as a marketing tool; it is simply wasting money.

The Role of Networking

Gurus in the world of career management call it 'networking'; those in the world of selling might call it 'making contacts'. Whatever the terminology, the principle is the same: to do business, people have to meet other people – in order to ask them questions, to give them information, to win their trust and simply to get to know them.

No one can exist in a ivory tower for all their lives; they have to meet and deal with people in order to live in the modern world. Most people leave the building of their networks largely to chance, starting with friends, neighbours and relatives, and then building from there with colleagues at work or people they come into contact with socially. This is a haphazard process, one in which people who start off well connected become even better connected, and those with less influence never catch up.

Someone who really understands the value of networking, however, and who has the nerve to do it, will target the people most likely to be useful to them either as customers, employees, employers, mentors or simply acquaintances. They will then find ways of getting to know them, winning their trust and exchanging information, probably with the intention eventually of buying something from them or selling something to them, or possibly simply to gain valuable information. Politicians are the most blatant users of this approach, but successful business people operate in exactly the same way.

To make the necessary contact with someone whom you want to build into your network, you have to persuade them to spend some of their valuable time with you. You may be able to do this simply on the strength of your personality or the proposition you are putting to them. You may be able to do it through an introduction from or by reference to some influential mutual contact. The chances are, however, that you will have none of these advantages.

If the target is someone you keenly want to reach, it is likely that they will be less enthusiastic about a meeting than you. There is little point, after all, in pursuing people who will get more from you than you can get from them (in that case they should be the ones chasing you). So you will have to find a way of catching their eye and luring them out to meet you. Once again, that brings us back to corporate entertainment, the bait you can attach to your hook.

'Corporate entertainment allows you to lobby people you need to reach,' says Eddie Hoare 'on your own territory and on your own terms.'

Sales Promotion Link

Corporate entertainment can be used as a sales promotional tool, in the same way as incentive gifts, but with scope for highly sophisticated add-ons.

Courvoisier, for instance, were looking for a way to win the loyalty of bar staff and publicans to encourage them to use their brand when asked by customers simply for 'a brandy'. They thought that corporate entertainment might be the key and started talking to Elegant Days.

After several meetings they evolved the concept of their Classic Club, offering members opportunities to book events like racing days, golfing days, days built round the Orient Express, theatre evenings and other sporting fixtures. In order to become members of the club, publicans and bar staff have to stock the product and, on booking an event, send a cork as proof. Some of the events feature special offers – for example, 'buy one place and a guest goes free'. The whole thing was packaged by Elegant Days but was branded to Courvoisier.

In this instance corporate entertainment has been used as a commodity in a marketing package with much broader and more sophisticated aims than simply meeting and getting to know people. The principles, however, are the same: providing people with experiences they couldn't easily obtain for themselves in any other way in order to build a relationship with them.

Chapter Summary

- Companies should use corporate entertainment because:
    - it can accurately fulfil a marketing brief;
    - it is precise and controllable;
    - it has a low wastage factor;
    - it provides an ideal selling atmosphere;
    - it can involve partners;
    - it provides measurable results;
    - it differentiates them from competitors;
    - it provides long-term memorability;
    - it is cost-effective;
    - it can target their best prospects, their existing customers;
    - it increases word-of-mouth recommendations;
    - it provides a sales aid to a salesforce;
    - it builds human relationships;
    - it assists in building networks;
    - it assists with sales promotions;
    - it allows companies to say 'please', 'thank you' and 'well done'.

Chapter 3

Targeting the Guests

A guest never forgets the host who has treated him kindly.'
Homer, *Odyssey*

The external guests which a company might be interested in entertaining will generally fall into three categories: existing customers, potential customers and other groups of people whom the company would like to get to know.

Existing Customers

Remember the golden rule of the previous chapter: there must be a reason. The fact that people are customers is not enough; you must have a purpose in inviting them, even if it is just to say thank you.

If saying thank you is the purpose, then it would be worth considering whether you can make a positive gain in some way as well. Can you, for instance, prepare guests for a forthcoming price rise, demonstrate a new product or introduce them to a new director?

You must decide on the purpose first, because only then will you be able to work out a profile of the people who can most profitably be invited. Once you have your profile, you can start to seek out the relevant people and then target them. Having a clear purpose will also help you in deciding on the most appropriate format for the event.

If it is to show off a new range of products, for instance,

then you know not to ask people who are very good customers but would never have a need for these particular goods. If it is to meet a new director, then you might be able to divide the client base up into those who would have something to do with this new person and those who wouldn't.

It may be that you can divide customers up on the basis of their financial value to your company as a first measure. Someone who spends millions with you, or has had a monthly account running for twenty years, is going to be of more value than someone who has made a one-off purchase of fairly low value – unless, of course, the purpose of the campaign is to turn one-off purchasers into regular customers.

Gathering Information

It may be that you know very little about your customers. If you do not have a direct salesforce but use direct-response advertising or some other impersonal means of marketing, you may know only the name of the company that buys from you, without even knowing what their business is. If you sell office chairs, for instance, and have a client called Smith and Co. that orders 100 new chairs a month from your catalogue, you may not have a contact name at Smith and Co.; if you have one, it may simply be someone in accounts who processes your invoices. Within Smith and Co. you want to reach the people who decide that new chairs need to be bought, and the people who then do the ordering, and possibly the people who agree the expenditure as well. All of them could be useful to you, all of them need to know about your company and your products. They need to know how financially sound you are, how keen you are to do business with them and how approachable and human you are; and they need to know why they should be buying new chairs more often and why they should be buying those chairs from you.

To start, therefore, you must gather as much information about your clients as you can in-house. That will mean talking to the sales department – which is the most likely to have in-depth information – the accounts department, the service department, and anyone else who may have come into contact with the client. If, for instance, you are selling computer installations, the people who spend time inside the client company setting the system up will be the most knowledgeable, yet they are unlikely to volunteer information unless asked.

Try to find out as much as you can about the client company, and about the people working in the project that led to the involvement of your company. Use any contacts you have to find out more. If you sell to one department or one company within a group, try to find out who else they know who buys the sorts of products or services you sell. It may be that the person you deal with has a boss who is in charge of a number of other potential buyers as well, and needs to be made aware of what you do.

All these various strands of information need to be pooled at some central location, preferably in the marketing department, so that they can be shared. It is no good one person in your company getting to know a client intimately but never sharing the knowledge with anyone else. What happens if that person decides to leave and takes the knowledge with them? What happens if there is some vital piece of information about the client – he is a golf fanatic or she is addicted to tennis – that could act as a hook, but the contact never thinks to mention it to anyone else?

It could be that someone in your company has social contact with someone in a client company outside working hours – their children go to the same school, they play squash together or are simply neighbours. While you can't expect your employees to divulge personal details about their friendships, they could be encouraged to talk about someone's special interests. It could help the friendship as well as the business relationship if your employee was able to invite their contact to a relevant and enjoyable event.

If, in the course of your research, you find a good client who is not known to you personally, it might be worth contacting them in a special way (at least by telephone, but preferably in person) – the call could come from someone in the after-sales service department rather than sales if you don't want to give the idea that you are intending to sell them something. It could be made as part of a wider customer care scheme, finding out what they think of the product and service you provide, whether they have any problems you can help with and so on. During the course of the conversation, however, you should be able to extract some personal information, something you can use to start building a long-term relationship.

Decision-makers and Influencers

You need to know who makes the purchasing decisions, who actually signs the order forms and who the influencers are.

Maybe the people you need to know are not right at the top of the company; maybe the chief executive actually agrees the order and signs the cheque but someone much further down the corporate ladder recommends which product to buy and which company to buy it from. In that case the influencers are the people you want to get to know and ensure that they think well of your company.

The fact that they are lower down the pecking order may work to your advantage, since they will be more accessible and more easily entertained. Chief executives who have climbed right to the top of the corporate ladder will have become relatively blasé about corporate hospitality, and will also have more pressures on their time. They will therefore be harder to tempt into accepting an invitation than someone who is still on their way up and hungry for new experiences, wanting to meet new people and keen to learn how to do their job better.

Potential Customers

It is bound to be harder to identify the best prospects for corporate entertainment from among all the companies or people that you would ideally like to supply than to sort through the limited number of clients that you already have.

Some companies are shy about using corporate entertainment for potential customers, believing that it is too obvious and can look like an outright bribe. It is interesting to note, however, that the corporate entertainment companies themselves use it extensively and find it highly successful. Whether or not it works comes down to the amount of research that goes into selecting the targets, and the ways in which invitations are presented.

In most industries there always has to be a certain amount of elimination involved before you have a workable list of prospects, but any marketing department with a long-term strategy always knows which companies it would most like to be working for and will have made some preliminary approaches.

The chances are that your sales people have already been in to see the most important prospects, or, if not, that you already have the names inside the prospect company that you have been writing to in the past. Now you need to refine the list down even further to those you would both like to work for and you believe would be likely to have an interest in getting to know you personally.

Be Realistic

You might dream of selling your services to IBM, Coca-Cola, ICI and Ford, but if you are being realistic you will probably have to admit that you are more likely at this stage of your development to get contracts from The John Doe Corporation, based in your local town. There is no point inviting a buyer from a major company if that company is still out of your league, because you have no hope of forming a mutually beneficial relationship with them. It would be like inviting the Queen of England or the First Lady of America to visit your local sports club when it would be more appropriate to invite the local mayor or the captain of a local football team.

This does not mean that you should not be aiming to sell to the biggest and best eventually; rather, it is just no good trying to move too fast if you are using corporate entertaining as a marketing tool. A precision marketing tool works only if it is completely practical. It is pointless fantasising, because unless the relationship is based in reality it won't work.

Find People Who Need to Know about You

There are potential customers who will be as keen to find out about your company as you are to tell them about it. If someone's job is to do nothing but buy in one product category, they will have a vested interest in being as well informed about that industry as possible. They need to know who has the best products, who is financially secure, who delivers on time, who has a good record at keeping staff, who is ambitious to grow and who is growing too fast. A good travel agent, for instance, should have a working knowledge of as many of the destinations and hotels that he or she is sending people to as possible. A machine-tool buyer needs to know which companies are producing the best products at any one time and who has new ideas in the pipeline. A restaurateur needs to find the best meat, fish and vegetables available. All these people have vested interests in meeting their suppliers and potential suppliers, finding the best ones and building relationships with them.

It is when both sides have something to gain from a relationship that corporate entertainment works best. Just as the secret of selling is finding product benefits that can be presented to the potential customer, so the secrets of successful corporate entertainment lie in demonstrating the benefits of attending to potential guests.

Entertaining Your Suppliers

In some cases the supplier is the one who needs to be wooed by the customer. If you have a brand-leading product that is in demand and you are allowing only certain authorised dealers or retailers to sell it, those dealers or retailers are going to want to ensure that you don't move the licence to their rivals. Similarly, those whom you don't supply will be anxious to demonstrate that they are worthy of your products and would market them as you would want, maintaining your image and giving you all the promotional back-up you feel you need.

It might be that you have a fashion shop, for instance, and want to sell some of the most exclusive designer names. Such people are very conscious of their image and would need to be convinced that you are somebody they can trust not to lower your standards and possibly spoil their image as a result.

Other Groups

Most of the other external groups will fall within the areas of your public relations and public affairs departments. The people in these departments will, as part of their jobs, know who the most influential people are in the area of press and politics, and should have formed relationships with them in the same way as the sales departments will have done with customers. It is then only a matter of finding out as much as possible about them as individuals, in order to know how to involve them more closely in the company's activities.

Just as with customers, it may be that people further down the hierarchy are most valuable – the journalist who is writing the copy that goes into a publication may be more useful than the editor, who, although a better 'name', has less to do with the actual article. It could also be that a freelance writer who contributes to a number of different outlets on a particular subject might be of even more value than staffers, who write only for one employer.

Only by getting to know each publication separately, however, will the public relations people be able to ascertain where the most useful contacts are to be found.

In the political arena the whole business of lobbying is about relationships and communications, and any lobbyist working successfully on behalf of their employer will already know a great deal about the politicians who are important to their company's interests.

Finding out about Them as People

Once you have ascertained which people are key to the success of your operation, you then need to find out all the information you can about them. Business is as much about relationships as any other aspect of life. People who get on well with others will always be the most successful at their jobs, and in order to get on well with other people you need to know something about them. You need to know their likes and dislikes, their hopes, dreams and ambitions, just in case you can make some of them come true.

The more you know about them, the more likely you are to be able to design an event that will attract them. Are they married? Do they have children? Do they like any particular sport? What sort of food do they like? Do they like opera or ballet? Do they have any other interests or hobbies?

This is not the sort of information that you can immediately demand of a customer, or indeed a journalist or politician – you can hardly give them a form to fill in asking for details of their private lives at your first sales call or during an interview. The overall picture will build up over a long period, though, and as a result of a number of meetings and informal conversations.

It may be too ambitious to hope to have more than the bare bones of the ideal information database when you first invite someone to an event. The important thing is to ensure that everyone in your company is aware of the need to find out information about the target group, record it and, most importantly, share it with the rest of the company. (Sales people in particular are notoriously keen to keep their contacts to themselves, and need to be given incentives in some way to input the data they collect into a central pool, especially as in most cases they will be the most prolific, and in some cases the only, source of information.)

Chapter Summary

- Decide on the purpose of the project.
- Decide on the profile of the targets who fit the purpose.
- Search out influencers as well as the decision-makers.
- Find out as much about them as possible.
- Decide what sort of event would be most suitable.
- Be realistic about who you invite.
- Find people who will want or need to know you better.
- Set up a central pool for all the information on targets.

Chapter 4

Making Sure Guests Attend

'Guests turn down more invitations to corporate hospitality functions than they accept.'

The Effectiveness of Corporate Hospitality,
BMSL Reports.

This is the most critical stage in any corporate entertainment plan, and it is the part that most host companies get wrong. Your goal is to persuade certain individuals to give up some of their valuable time to join you. Once they are with you, you then have to find ways of making the event as productive and enjoyable for everyone concerned as possible. It is attracting people in the first place that is the hardest part.

The more important and valuable the individuals are, the harder it is going to be to tempt them to take time away from their desks or their homes to be with you. They will have more pressures on their time and more people inviting them to events, so they will be less easily impressed by anything you have to offer.

Hitting The 'Hot Button'

Attempting to land useful guests at an event is just like fishing, and if you don't choose exactly the right bait, the big fish you are after will keep on swimming past while you end up catching something small and inedible, or nothing at all. You have got, as they say in the industry, to hit someone's 'hot button'. You must find out exactly what really turns them on and then make them an offer they can't refuse.

This means that you have to know at least a little about them, and preferably a lot. If you know, for instance, that they go to the races every week, then it will be no great incentive to offer a simple day at the races. However, if you were to suggest a day in the owner's enclosure, and a walk of the course before the race with a leading jockey, that might be a different matter.

If they are keen golfers, a day on the golf course is not going to be a big deal, but if you could arrange for them to go to a course that is so exclusive they have never been able to get there themselves, or find a professional player whom they admire to give them a few pointers, again, that would be attractive.

If they travel all the time for their work, they may be sick and tired of certain locations. It is up to you to find places they have always wanted to go to but have never been sent to by their company.

'You could be inviting someone to the best tennis tournament in the world,' says David Tonnison, 'and wondering why they keep refusing, when a little research would show that that person is a dedicated opera buff who would accept virtually any invitation in that category.'

You have to be able to give people something they can't get for themselves, and it may take a combination of attractions to find the hot button.

Overcoming Barriers

As well as finding people's hot buttons, you also need to overcome their barriers to accepting. It may be that one of your targets is under pressure at work and feels guilty about seeming to take time off. In that case you will need either to give the event a high work content (for example, allow them to sample a product they need to know about for their job, or to meet some people who are important or useful to them) or to arrange it out of working hours, whether in the evening or at a weekend. It may be that you need to do both.

Another target might feel guilty about spending too little time with their family, in which case you will need to invite the family as well. That could mean finding out what their partner likes to do and arranging something around that (a chief executive's wife might love opera, or a husband might love sailing). If they have children, then you could arrange some sort of family event at a weekend. If you can involve your target's family, you are nearly always going to please them and make them well disposed to accepting an invitation.

Suppose, for instance, that you can arrange tickets to an important football match for a father and son and include meeting some of the players and going on to the pitch before the match. The father is going to see himself looking very good in his son's eyes, and, having arranged it for him, you can be there to share the moment.

Perhaps you want to invite your target somewhere that will involve a flight but you know they are fed up with travelling. If you just tell them the destination, they might refuse, but if you hired a private plane or arranged first-class tickets it might make all the difference.

Give People an Opportunity to Boast

One of the hooks few people can resist is an event that gives them an opportunity to boast. Some will be more subtle than others, but most of us like to feel we are outdoing our rivals.

People want to feel important, so important that they don't just get invited for a night out in New York or London but are taken to the most exclusive hotels and restaurants, places they have never been before but know to be good – places they can be fairly sure that other people they mix with will not have visited. They can boast about private planes and first-class tickets, eating at palaces and stately homes, and meeting famous people. To go game-shooting on an estate in Scotland is one thing; to be sitting next to the lord of the manor at lunch afterwards turns it into some-thing else altogether. Seeing a major star perform in Las Vegas is great; if you can eat with them afterwards, or play a round of golf with them, you will really have something to tell the kids about when you get home.

It is important to judge your target's level of sophisti-cation. If you get it wrong, pitching the tone too high or too low, you will either intimidate or insult them, and both ways you will lose them.

If you offer an invitation to meet Prince Charles at a polo match, you will attract some people but make others feel you are branding them as social climbers. If you set the tone differently, inviting them to a private lunch at a polo match, with the opportunity to watch the game and have Prince Charles explaining some of the finer points, you will appeal to a different type of target.

You also need to judge the relative importance of the target. Would it, for instance, be worth your while taking a whole day to go round a golf course with one or two guests? And again, would it be useful to take ten prospects and spend the same on them as you might if you invited 100 people to something less expensive?

Getting the Invitations Right

According to Philippa Bovey:

> Getting the RSVPs is the hardest part of the operation. Most companies can answer all the 'who', 'what', 'when', 'why', and 'where' questions and they are fine at selecting the venue,

but when it comes to the implementation stage, they fail because they think that all they have to do is send out the letters of invitation and leave it at that. What they don't understand is that they have to go through an 'invitation process' and they have to do it well, with clever design ideas, plenty of time and a follow-up plan if they want to be successful.

This is where a lot of people go wrong and is why the average recipient of corporate invitations is thought to decline seven for every one accepted.

The most common mistake is to leave everything to the last minute. If you send out invitations to an event that is only a few weeks away, you are going to have a high failure rate. To begin with, the most important people will have their diaries full for months in advance. Secondly, they will feel insulted, believing that you have approached them only as a last resort because you weren't able to get the people you really wanted.

Chas Wheeler, an independent agent who has been in the business a number of years, has found:

> Some companies make the mistake of taking a marquee somewhere and then allocating a certain number of spaces to each of their regions. The regional managers, who have not been involved in the initial planning stages and feel no ownership for the project, give it very low priority and don't invite anyone until a month beforehand. By that time the targets' diaries are full and they are insulted to have been asked at the last moment. The host is then left with a half-empty marquee and wonders why. There has to be someone who is in charge from start to finish, who is determined to make it work.

Philippa Bovey again:

> If you do want to reach people on a regional basis, it is usually better to arrange something locally for each region. It may be that the most important targets can be got to one central location for something spectacular, but that it would be more cost-effective when talking to the next layer of targets to take the entertainment to them rather than the other way round.

You need, therefore, to plan the whole thing months in advance, whether you start with a casual invitation issued in the course of a conversation or a formal, printed invitation.

Imagine, for instance, the target is worth several million a year in orders to you and, during the course of a conversation, you discover that they have always wanted to go sailing in a certain sort of boat. You could casually say, 'Oh well, we must arrange to do that one weekend.' You can then go away and find out more about the boat in question, where to hire one, where to sail it and how many people should be involved.

Armed with that information, you can then decide whether to keep the event individual for this one person only, or to combine it with one or two other targets. If, for instance, you have a number of clients who are keen on sailing, you could arrange a race of some sort.

You can now call the original target back, or write, inviting them to sail with you in the boat that they were talking about. You can then go on to contact any others who might be interested, using just the same informal manner.

If this is a personal dream, you can be sure that your target will put the date in their diary and not allow anything else to push it out.

Alternatively, if you are arranging an event that will involve a number of targets, you might need to take a more formal approach at the start, with invitations cleverly worded to make the event seem different from all the others they may have been offered by your competitors, and laying out the advantages to be gained from coming, as well as the purpose.

The advantages could simply be a pleasant day out somewhere and the chance to get to know some new people. They could equally well be the opportunity of tasting the food of a famous chef, sampling some famous wine vintages, meeting a group of their peers from rival companies, staying at a famous hotel, getting the best seats at some desirable sporting or entertainment event, driving a Formula One racing car, riding a racehorse, going across country on the latest dune buggy, test-driving the latest sports car or hang-gliding from a local mountain. The possibilities are endless.

As Chas Wheeler says:

> You need to think creatively. It is no good just asking someone to the races if they get invited by several people every year. If you book a top jockey, however, and send the invitation from him or her, promising that they will be passing on a few tips after lunch, you have changed the nature of the invitation.

What If They Pass It on?

The danger with the less personal approach is that your target may simply hand the invitation on to a colleague, and that colleague may be someone who is of no use to your company at all. Worse still, they might hand it to a friend or member of their family who has no connection at all with your industry.

'If you aren't careful,' says Eddie Hoare, 'you can end up with rent-a-crowd, which is no use to anyone.'

You need to plan for this eventuality. Work out who you would be willing to accept as a substitute and who you wouldn't. It may be that someone else in the target company is even better than the person you originally approached, but if this is the case, you have started off on the wrong foot by demonstrating that they were not your first choice.

If you find that the invitation has been accepted on behalf of the target company by someone unknown to you, you would be wise to contact your original choice and ask them if they are quite sure this person would really enjoy the event. If you are able to say that you chose the venue or the event because of something specific your original choice said to you, and that really they were the people you wanted to invite, you will be on much firmer ground than if you merely complain about getting someone less influential.

If the person you invited is insistent that the second person will enjoy the event and benefit from getting to know the hosts, then you may have to accept their judgement. First, however, you need to find out as much as possible about the person who has accepted your invitation, and this will mean talking to them direct. If your research reveals that they do not meet your criteria, you can then go to them direct and explain that the event was arranged specifically for the person named on the invitation and that you really don't think they will get much from it. Apologise for the misunderstanding and, if they seem upset, suggest that you meet up at your premises to get to know each other better, and see if there is anything else that could be arranged.

If they are genuinely interested in your company, they will take you up on this offer and you will be able to find out more about them and start building a relationship on solid foundations. The chances are that they will cry off at this stage. It is vital, of course, that you handle any case like this very tactfully, since it is impossible to judge what hidden influence that person might have within your target company, and you may even end up building a better relationship with this new person than you had with the original target.

An added danger if the invitation has been handed on is that the person who now has it is less likely to feel obliged to turn up if the event is inconvenient or if they change their minds. You need, therefore, to have some personal contact with them during the invitation process, so that you can check they are coming a day or two before.

The best way, though, to avoid any of these pitfalls is to do enough research before issuing the invitation to ensure that it will be personal to the invitee, hitting their 'hot button' so hard that they will guard it with their life.

Following up the Invitation

As your initial invitation will have to be sent several months in advance in order to get into your target's diary, you are going to have to ensure that you keep up their enthusiasm as the day draws near. That does not mean pestering them unnecessarily, but it does mean keeping in contact.

If you have anything new about the day to tell them, that will give you an excuse for writing. If not, then you must make a plan of all the things they will need – for instance, entry tickets, passes for their cars or maps showing how to get to the location and where to park. They may also need advice like 'wear sensible shoes' or 'dress formally', depending on the event and the rules of the venue.

All these communications should be coordinated to ensure that the material you send is well presented, relevant, highly personalised and helpful, without any repetition.

Someone in the host company must be in charge of the guest list and keep track of the names of those who have accepted and those who have refused. They will then have the responsibility of calling people who have not responded and persuading them to attend.

Philippa Bovey comments:

Because this is such a young industry you find that different people are responsible for the entertainment arrangements in every company. While some large companies have dedicated people or departments, others let the chairman's secretary handle it, others hand it over to the public relations department or the marketing director or the business development manager. In some cases it is given to a temporary secretary to handle, and that is when the real problems start. Someone junior is much more likely to fall foul of the cowboy operator selling the 'last-minute bargain', and much less likely to have any interest in the invitation process. Companies need to realise that these decisions should be taken at a high level and handled by people who understand the marketing process thoroughly.

If the event involves a certain number of prebooked seats that need to be filled if they are not to be wasted, then there should be a reserve list to bring into play should any gaps occur. There must be sufficient time to make these secondary invitations look planned and not last-minute panics – nobody likes to feel that they have been invited only to make up the numbers; if that is the impression you give, then you may have actually damaged the potential relationship rather than enhanced it.

Everyone on the reserve list must still be a relevant target, and it is better to waste the seat, and consequently make the event seem even more exclusive for the people who do attend, than to invite someone who does not fit in with the rest of the group.

A day or two before the actual event, make one last personal call to check that everyone is happy with the arrangements, and knows where to go and what to bring. If there are any problems at this stage, you can sort them out. If people are worried about transport, you can arrange to have them picked up; if they are worried about getting home, you can arrange for them to have overnight accommodation somewhere convenient. These last-minute touches will make all the difference, pushing home the fact that you really want people to come, and making it hard for them to let you down. Right from the beginning you should budget for the possibility that these extra expenses will crop up.

Other Guests

It may well be that the guests can be of use to one another, as well as to you, the host. Just as at a private party you mix people you think will be of interest to each other, so a skilful corporate entertainer will pick guests from different areas of expertise but with matching needs.

As Eddie Hoare explains:

> If you arrange a night out at the theatre and you invite an accountant, a lawyer and an architect, it may well be that they will be able to do business with one another. Think how grateful they will be to you then.
>
> As with a private dinner party, you need to pick people who will like each other. If you have a friend who is an ardent Communist and another who verges on Fascism, it is probably not a good idea to ask them to the same party – unless you are particularly hoping for a lively debate.

And Philippa Bovey feels:

> For people to have a good time, they need to be with people they like. It is up to the host company to ensure that they know enough about each of the guests to be able to mix and match them successfully. Ideally they will have built up a database on their life-styles that not only has details like the names and ages of their children and their spouse's birthday, but also lists their sporting and other interests, their pet likes and dislikes, so that they can ensure they will have something in common with other guests.

It is important, therefore, that the host company knows exactly where all the guests are coming from. Chas Wheeler remembers handling an event for a newspaper which involved a group of guests at a football match. What the host hadn't told him was that although most of the guests were corporate clients, some were competition prize-winners, who turned up complete with scarves and rattles. They all ended up in the same room with both sides feeling extremely uncomfortable.

To ensure that someone attends your event, you must make it plain to them from the start that you have arranged it with them in mind, that you sincerely want them to come, that they are important to you, and that your main aim is to make the time spent with you as memorable and comfortable for them as possible.

Chapter Summary

- Recognise that getting an RSVP is the hardest part of the operation.
- Discover your targets' hot buttons.
- Anticipate their barriers to acceptance and plan to overcome them.
- Look for ways of involving partners and families.
- Provide targets with opportunities to boast.
- Take trouble to get the invitations right.
- Get the invitations out well in advance, with approximate timings.
- Set up an invitation process, and have someone in sole charge of it.
- Remind people as often as necessary.
- Supply them with maps, itineraries and other information.
- Speak to them all personally within forty-eight hours of the event to check that they have no problems.

Chapter 5

Entertaining Internally

Those who work in the field of staff motivation always tend to stress their difference from the corporate hospitality sector, which is directed at customers, potential customers and other external audiences. In fact, they share many of the same goals and benefit from a number of the same techniques.

Companies are now very aware of the importance of the people who work for them. Departments that were once referred to as 'Personnel' are now known as 'Human Resources', which means exactly what it says. In a world where many products are now identical, the companies that can provide the most 'added value' are the ones that win the customers. This basically means the companies that provide good service, and the only way to provide good service is to recruit good people, and then train and motivate them effectively so that they understand what the company philosophies are and want to put them actively into practice.

Once you have recruited good people, you then need to develop them and encourage them to stay, which means making the working environment as stimulating as possible and making them feel part of the corporate culture.

To bring this about you have to build relationships with people, just as you do with customers. You have to find out what it is they want from their working lives, and help them to achieve their goals. You need to know what turns them on and what turns them off; in other words, their hot buttons are just as important as your clients'. You must also show how much you value them, making it clear that they are vital to the success of the company and creating as convivial and social an atmosphere as possible within the workplace.

Oiling the Wheels of Change

As well as realising the importance of their human resources, most companies are also acknowledging that they will have to make changes more often and faster than ever before if they are to survive and prosper in the marketplaces of the future. For this to be possible, everyone needs to know about possible changes as soon as possible, because otherwise they will still be set in their old ways when the time comes to adapt and move on. The most effective way to convey the necessary messages is to meet people and explain things face to face in a friendly environment.

Traditionally, companies might have used their newsletters to talk about changes, but that method cannot be relied upon any more. Paper communication is just information-giving; it does not motivate people to change. If a company has something important to put across, it is worth taking the time to do it properly, and this means building relationships of mutual understanding with the targets of the communication, meeting them and talking to them.

Making Meetings, Conferences and Seminars Memorable

The need to convey information effectively has given rise to the meeting, conference and seminar industries, all of which provide opportunities for corporate entertainment.

Used creatively, they can ensure that key messages are heard, remembered and acted upon.

If you are organising conferences at which management simply stands on a stage and talks at delegates, you have moved only one step on from the newsletter. If, however, you create situations in which there is genuine interaction and explanation, you have a better chance of making a difference to people's attitudes.

Most events like conferences involve some sort of catering or social input. If you are going to have to feed the delegates anyway, why not take the opportunity to do something memorable? It is simply a question of looking for ways to make the social side of the event work for you. Rather than looking for the cheapest and most convenient way to shovel meals into everyone and then sending them back to the auditorium, a lunch can be turned into something exciting and different, perhaps by the choice of venue, or menu, or by the way it is served. If there is an opportunity for an evening meal, the scope for theming and entertainment is considerably broader since time restrictions are less rigid.

Equally, a two-day conference in a hotel might be 100 per cent more effective if extended by one day and designed to include a day of team games or sports (see Chapter 10).

Unlocking Creativity

An international computer consultancy takes its entire workforce away for a weekend every year. With a dozen offices around the world, the staff have few opportunities to meet colleagues from different countries face to face. One year, for instance, they flew 400 people from all over the world to Amsterdam and Rotterdam airports, where they were met by coaches and taken to a converted monastery in the forests near Veldhoven.

They arrived on a Friday and were given a drinks reception and dinner with no speeches on the first evening. Sports facilities were available and people were able to meet and get to know one another, particularly people who until then had spoken only on the telephone.

On the Saturday they were given a list of about a dozen 'breakout groups' discussing different topics. Two or three people had been asked to put together each group and act as session leaders. Each group was run four times during the day, in order to enable people to go into groups that were dealing with subjects outside their own specific areas of knowledge, perhaps two of each. The idea was to generate ideas through discussion.

There were also standard presentations from senior management on the issues facing the company and how they intended to tackle them, plus talks on the future of the business.

On Sunday morning each of the national teams spent thirty minutes doing whatever they wanted in the way of a show to entertain the rest of the party. The audience voted for their favourites and the winners got to host the next annual get-together. All through the weekend there were sporting and social events.

By the end of an event like this, where everyone feels they have made a contribution, friendships and relationships are bound to have developed and improved, and the company will have been able to get across its corporate message in a convivial and receptive atmosphere.

Theming Incentive Campaigns

With creative flair, companies can create themed incentive campaigns with a corporate entertainment content that will catch the imagination of almost anyone. Elegant Days, for instance, has created a 'Win an Island' campaign, culminating in a winner actually owning their own island in Scotland. Eddie Hoare explains:

The campaign would be launched with a promotional lunch on an island somewhere. The first level of prize-winners would then get a long weekend in the Isle of Wight or the Scilly Isles. Then there would be a week on a Caribbean island for the next level of achievement, possibly one of the private ones. Then the final winner gets their own island.

Although it sounds extremely expensive, an island of this sort might well cost less than a luxury car, but with far more public relations potential. 'These sorts of islands are not really for living on,' admits Hoare. 'They are more for buying and selling and boasting about. But then, giving people something to boast about is one of the main objectives of corporate entertainment.'

Motivating Staff to Build Relationships with Customers

We have already established how important it is for your customers to form personal relationships with the people working in your company, in order to gain their loyalty and encourage them to recommend you to others. To achieve that, however, you need to ensure that the people they deal with stay with you for as long as possible, and are as highly motivated as you are to get to know the customers and to provide them with the products and services they need. This holds for everyone in the company.

All too often internal motivation programmes go as far as offering incentives for the salesforce to improve their figures and then no further. There is no point in building a wonderful and exclusive relationship between a sales person and a customer if the bulk of the day-to-day handling of the account is done by someone else. A sales call may take place only once every few months or years, whereas service engineers, accounts departments or delivery staff may be in contact with customers every day or week. A mechanic in a garage who builds a relationship of mutual trust with a valued customer is more likely to keep that customer coming back to the garage than the sales person who sold them the car in the first place. Customers like to feel that they are being looked after once they have made a purchase, not that they have just been sold to; they like to feel that they have access to experts who will be able to help when it is necessary. Only highly motivated staff will be able to provide such a service.

A successful company culture, therefore, is one that involves all employees, making them feel glad they work for the company and keen to do the best they can on the company's behalf. Corporate entertainment is a highly effective method of achieving these goals.

The Need for Two-way Communication

Just as the management of the company needs to know and understand the employees, so employees need to know and understand the people who make the decisions in the company. They have to understand how and why the decisions are made and, if possible, respect the people who make them. This can happen only if they are given a chance to get to know the managers in a setting away from the workplace where they can talk as equals, each explaining their problems and goals, and the realities of their respective situations.

In simplified terms, the managing director can explain why the company needs to increase production, and the machine worker can explain why new machinery is needed in order to do that. If a written order to increase production comes down from on high, the machine worker will simply complain about the unfairness of it all, and will assume that management is out of touch with the realities of the shop floor. If, however, that worker feels part of the same team as management, knowing that their opinion was sought and listened to, and understanding the reason behind the request, the chances are they will do all in their power to comply with it.

It is unrealistic in a large company to imagine that everyone can get close to the managing director, but there are always ways for the decision-makers to meet and talk with the people their decisions will effect, and vice versa.

If there is some sort of social interchange between all the different levels in a company, everyone feels that they are part of the decision-making process; everyone feels that they have had an input (and in a perfect situation they will truly have made an input, either by talking through their ideas or by simply providing information that helps managers to make the right decisions).

For all this interchange of information to happen, people must meet in situations that are conducive to relaxed and open discussion. A well-planned corporate entertainment will provide exactly that situation.

Excuses for a Party

An entertainment event can be linked in with any number of other activities. It can be a gala dinner at the end of a conference or an activity day used as part of a training programme; a prize dangled at the end of an incentive programme or at any stage during it when a motivational message needs to be got across; a celebration to mark the opening of a new office or the launch of a new company image; or simply a Christmas party or a chance for people within the company to get to know their fellow workers on an informal basis.

It can also be an opportunity to meet partners and children of the people you work with. Knowing someone's family completely alters your perception of that person and your relationship to them; you are immediately able to see them from a different perspective. Any 'front' or 'act' they put on at work will change when they are with their families, and in order to build a strong and lasting relationship at work, it helps to know the whole individual, not just the persona who comes to work in a suit or overalls.

Suiting the Event to the Guests

The main rule to bear in mind when choosing an event for staff is to think of something that will suit them as well as you. It is no good dragging the whole company out to the golf course just because it happens to be the chairman's favourite game. Nor is it necessarily useful to take everyone to a sporting event just because you are sponsoring it and therefore have access to free tickets.

You need to start by researching what it is that the potential guests would like to do, and what they cannot organise for themselves. You need to invite them all individually, just as you would a client, tempting and persuading them to attend, even though you know that they will find it hard to say no (unlike clients in a similar position). Simply telling people that an event has been arranged and they are expected to be there is not enough; they must feel that you have designed it specifically for them and that you really want them to come because you are planning to thank them for something, or talk to them about something, or simply to get to know them better.

There must be a reason for the event that the guests can understand; otherwise it is simply a 'work do' and as much of a chore as a meeting or a business lunch.

Participative sports and activities can be effective for staff entertainment, since in most cases the people involved already know one another and have probably already built up friendly rivalries that can be used to light-hearted ends. Chances to beat the boss at some entertaining activity, or for the accounts department to show the sales department what they are made of, can work as constructive team-building and cooperative exercises.

It is vital, of course, that any rivalry is kept friendly, and that the event does not simply widen the gap between two departments, or cause someone to fail in the eyes of their colleagues. Once again, you need to know a lot about all the individuals involved, and their relationships with one another, before you make any decisions.

Some events will have to be organised on such a large scale that it is impossible to hope to match exactly the preferences of all the guests. If an event involves several hundred people, there will be some there who hate that type of function. Provided that the majority are excited and looking forward to it, you should still go ahead; but you must be aware of which people are likely to feel out of place or embarrassed, and which might spoil other people's fun with sarcasm or cynicism. These people have to be looked after particularly well.

Say, for instance, that you decide to throw a fancy dress ball. Anyone who is likely to have trouble getting into the spirit of the event needs to receive some sort of personal call when the concept is first decided on, explaining why the event is happening and how they could help to make it a success. As soon as they feel they are involved and important, their attitude will begin to change. You also need to ensure that the event does not cause the guests too much inconvenience, worry or expense. The idea is to entertain them and put them in a positive frame of mind, not a negative one. If they are worried about getting the right costume, then make sure there are costumes available and people on hand to help with the choosing. If they are worried about how to get to and from the event, lay on travel for them and explain how it will work. People's enjoyment of events can often be marred by the most trivial of hang-ups and it is the organiser's responsibility to anticipate possible problems and circumvent them with clear explanations. As with all corporate entertainment, it is attention to detail that is important.

Chapter Summary

- Only people can add value to products. You need, therefore, to recruit the best and motivate them well.
- Only by getting to know your employees can you learn how to motivate them.
- People want to be involved in their company's culture, provided that they are made to feel comfortable with it.
- People need to believe they are valued by their employers.
- Effective communications with employees oils the wheels of change.
- Creative use of corporate entertainment at meetings and conferences will help to make key messages memorable.
- Companies must motivate staff to want to build relationships with clients.
- Look for ways to improve face-to-face communication at all levels.
- Use participative events to build team spirit, not to widen gaps. Never allow people to be seen to fail.

Chapter 6

Making the Choices

Once you have compiled as much information as possible about the people you want to target through entertainment, you then have to make a number of choices in order to create exactly the right event to suit their tastes and your goals.

Where?

Conrad Hilton has been famously quoted as saying that their are three crucial ingredients in creating a successful hotel: 'Location, location and location'. The same could be said of corporate entertainment. If the setting is wrong, people will be turned off and will not come, meaning that you have lost even before the start.

As Chas Wheeler says:

> There aren't many events that make it worthwhile for people to travel more than a few hours. It would be much better, for instance, to organise a number of regional events, if your business is widespread, than to expect everyone to travel to one point. In the long run it will also be cheaper as well as more effective.

There are a number of factors to play off against one another here – for instance, convenience against excitement. An event that all the guests could get to from their homes within half an hour might attract a high acceptance rate. Alternatively, a distant and exotic location might act as the hook to catch the big fish. People do, on the whole, find the idea of travel daunting, but at the same time it is felt to be stimulating, provided that the destination is one they want to visit and all the other ingredients in the mix are right.

To a large degree your choice of location depends on the life-styles of the people you are approaching. If they travel throughout Europe or America in the course of their work, they are unlikely to be excited by the prospect of a visit to Paris or New York (although their partners might, as we will discuss in a moment). They might, however, be tempted by Hawaii or the Far East if they are based in Europe, and the Great Barrier Reef or London and Paris if they are based in America.

These are exaggerated examples, and in most cases the cost of long-haul travel will be out of the question anyway, but a famous location that is two or three hours' travelling time from their base might lure people who are not particularly concerned about being back in their own beds by midnight.

Just as you have to weigh up the pros and cons of distance, you also have to look at different types of location. Are your guests more likely to enjoy a city break or time off in the country? Again, it will depend upon their life-styles. If they spend most of their time living in the suburbs of Birmingham or Los Angeles, they might appreciate the opportunity to get some fresh air and exercise in the peace of a country house somewhere or a famous vineyard. If they spend their lives in small, provincial towns, then they might like the idea of heading into Las Vegas or London for the bustle, excitement and glamour.

For most organisers, of course, the choices are far more mundane than this. They will start by looking at the convenience aspect, since travelling time is one of the major turn-offs for most corporate guests. This means looking at motorway layouts and access to airports; working out the relative merits of private planes as against scheduled ones, trains and taxis as against private cars; and looking at venues within a certain radius that are physically capable of handling the event and making decisions based on the most fundamental practicalities.

Pricing

Simon Morris, managing director of the Profile Partnership, has found it surprising how many clients never bother to negotiate prices with suppliers:

> Once you have a short-list of possible venues, for instance, price will be an important factor in making the final choice, and you should start asking some sensible questions. Most hotels, for instance, will provide discounts for weekend breaks, and if pressed will extend those weekends to cover Thursday to Monday. If it is a group of any size, they may well offer further discounts, cutting the costs in half, or more. It is always worth investigating ways of cutting costs if you can do so without affecting the quality of the event.

As Chas Wheeler says:

> There seem to be two distinct sectors in the market. There are the mass-market customers, who do not want to spend a lot and still seem to be happy with the basic packages that are on offer. Then there are people who want to buy quality, which means everything from good service and food to extra space and comfort. The difference in price between the two standards is not that great compared to the differences in standards. I believe that anyone who is at a corporate entertainment event should be able to expect a level of service comparable with the best restaurants and hotels. There really aren't any excuses for anything less.

When?

Next comes the choice of when to hold the event. We have already examined the need to plan well in advance, so that guests have plenty of time to fit functions into their diaries and organisers have plenty of time to make sure everything is done well. You also have to decide whether you are going to hold your events at the same time as everyone else (which generally means during the summer months, when the weather is more likely to be reliable and there are a number of regular sporting and social fixtures), or aim for a season of the year when there will be less competition for the guests' time.

Around Christmas, for instance, everyone has more invitations to functions than they know what to do with, and they are probably more concerned with the organisation of their own office party than with attending anyone else's. Two or three months either side of the holiday, however, in the flatter months of the autumn and spring, there are great opportunities for sending out invitations that will catch people's attention.

Sometimes an out-of-season event can be highly imaginative. Elegant Days, for instance, has in the past taken people to Norway in the winter to drive on the ice, ski cross-country or fish through the ice (using chain-saws to cut the holes).

Chas Wheeler again:

> In some cases the objectives of the event will dictate the timing. It may be, for instance, that you have a product range that sells mainly in the summer months, which means that you need to get the orders in September the year before. If your buying cycle is that predictable, you can fit the event in at the moment when it is likely to have the most dramatic effect on sales. Likewise, you might be able to time it to coincide with an advertising or sales promotion campaign.

Once you have decided on the time of year, you then have to pick the time of the week. Do you want to cut into your guests' weekends or their working weeks? Most people have a conscience about spending too much time away from work unless they can be sure that the event will be good for business in some way. They may allot them-selves a few days a year for this sort of activity, but you will need to have a strong hook to pull someone out of the office during the day otherwise. The evenings can work well, although people are conscious of the need to get home to their partners, and partners may find it difficult to be out on a weekday evening when there is work the next day.

The weekends provide a lot of scope for entertainment, but just as people feel guilty about being away from work during the week, most hard-working and successful people also feel guilty about neglecting their families. If you are going to use a weekend, therefore, you must invite part-ners, and probably children as well.

For How Long

It might sound very generous to invite a group of guests to some glamorous location for a whole weekend, but unless everyone knows each other very well you may be treading on dangerous ground. Some of them may turn down the invitation for fear of being trapped with a group of people they don't like. It is safer to limit an event to one night until you are confident that people are going to get on, and that you have enough activities to keep them occupied all the time. In most cases a one-day event will be more than enough, and a night should be included only for logistical reasons.

When to Invite the Family

The best way to catch anyone's attention is to invite their whole family to an event that all of them want to attend. (That could mean a trip to Disneyworld at the top of the scale, a tailor-made funfair or a specific event that will appeal, such as hot-air ballooning.) The costs, however, will soon mount up and you may well find that for some companies a family entertainment image just isn't suitable.

It all depends on who you are inviting. If your target guests are all chief executives and chairmen of major companies, the chances are that their children have already flown the nest and they themselves would rather spend their weekends on wonderful golf courses or ski slopes, shopping in capital cities or simply relaxing in top hotels.

If, however, you are aiming at middle management, with an age profile in their thirties and forties, then the chances are that they will have children and be delighted with anyone who finds a way to entertain them for a day. If you can relieve the parents of the children for even a few hours, you stand a good chance of being able to hold the parents' attention for any other message that you want to put across.

Traditionally, however, children are not included in corporate entertainment, and the question is simply whether to invite partners or not. In the past, most corporate entertainers decided against partners on the majority of invitations. The decision was generally made on the grounds of costs – the accountants simply couldn't see the sense in doubling the costs in order to entertain people who, they believed, contributed nothing to the company's bottom line.

That trend has changed with the growing realisation that partners do contribute a great deal to the bottom line, if only by motivating the targets to work harder in order to achieve certain goals, and it is now more common for partners to be included in the corporate entertainment plan. The main reason is targeting. Although the inclusion of partners doubles the number of guests, it also more than doubles the impact of the event. In many cases an event simply would not happen without partners, or would be a patent sham (like a ball or a romantic cruise).

If, therefore, you have decided that you can afford to entertain 100 people, you have the choice of either inviting

100 targets without their partners or 50 couples. Although the former option will reach a wider spread of your target audience, it will have far less impact. Someone whose partner comes with them will be more impressed, will have a better time and will have an added reason to feel that the host is truly interested in them and so develop a feeling of loyalty.

In many cases finding an event that pleases their partner will be easier than finding one for the actual target. Most of the primary targets for corporate entertainment are successful business people, and since they are frequently high earners, and well travelled, they are likely to be blasé about many of the things most people would find exciting. Often their partners have had fewer opportunities to experience the sort of events that companies are able to put on, and will therefore be more easily attracted. Your key target will then be happy to attend an event that they might, if invited on their own, have turned down, in order to please their partner. The primary target, for instance, may travel to New York several times a month, and will not be particularly excited at the prospect of spending an evening out on Broadway, while their partner, who has never been there, may have a very different attitude. In such a situation the primary target may well jump at the opportunity your corporate entertainment invitation provides simply because it will please their partner.

This equation has traditionally worked well because the majority of primary targets have been men. The waters have become muddier in recent years as more women are reaching positions of power and influence in the business world. It is now quite possible that the partner of your primary target is just as successful and hard to impress as the target themselves, whatever their gender. In these cases, however, the target couple will often be pleased to be invited to something they can share, since their life-styles are bound to keep them apart for much of the time. (It may also be that both partners are good targets for the host on purely business grounds. If the wife of their best customer, for instance, is a powerful lawyer, she might well be a contact the company would like to cultivate.)

In situations where the primary targets are mostly one gender, the inviting of partners has another advantage. Men tend to behave very differently if there is a mix of sexes in a group. They are more likely to relax and to mix better socially, and less likely to drink too much or become aggressively competitive. An all-female group is also likely to be more competitive and less relaxed, and there is a danger with either gender that on their own they will talk only about business – which is not the point of the exercise. The group dynamics will therefore be much easier to manage and much more effective with a balance of the sexes – a secret skilful dinner party hostesses have known for centuries. Most people, whether they admit it or not, enjoy the company of the opposite sex at social gatherings.

If partners have a good time at a corporate entertainment event, and meet and like the hosts, the chances are that they will talk about them to your target at home. They will inquire if you are still doing business with them, and if not why not. They will keep the host's name alive long after the guest at the '100 key targets' event has forgotten all about it.

It is always better to organise an event well for a few people than averagely for a lot. Effectively including partners adds to the quality of the occasion and to its power as a marketing tool. Consequently it is a more accurate form of targeting.

What to Do?

The range of options available for entertaining guests is now vast. You could simply invite them to lunch somewhere special, or to a sporting or cultural event. Alternatively, you could make the occasion more participative, be it wine-tasting, archery, falconry or driving a Formula One racing car.

The choice is going to be guided partly by costs, but mainly by the profile of your targets. You need to know what they have done before. It is no good inviting them to the races or a top golf tournament if they go regularly themselves, or have been invited to the same events every year for the past ten years.

People who receive a number of corporate entertainment invitations may use them as a way of getting to see their favourite sporting event each year, regardless of who invites them. They may not even remember the name of the host company once they have left. If they are too familiar with the venue, there is also the danger that they will wander off and do their own thing once they have got in free on your invitation. You need, therefore, to pick something that hits their hot button but that they haven't done before or would be unable to arrange for themselves.

If you are making corporate entertainment a regular part of your marketing mix, you also have to decide whether you are going to use the same event every year or find new things to do each time. If a particular event is a success one year, it is tempting to repeat the exercise the following year, and the majority of companies do just that. This may be an enjoyable exercise, but you run the risk that it will lose some of its appeal through familiarity. Such a decision can be taken only by a host who knows how good a relationship he or she has with their targets, and can therefore be confident that a repeat is something they would truly enjoy. You will also need to ensure that the experience is slightly better for them each year; the worst thing they could say once home is, 'Well, it wasn't as good as last year.'

The other danger for the regular user is getting caught in a spiral of ever-increasing cost. If you try too hard to impress your targets with the extravagance and generosity of your invitation the first year, you are going to have to do something even more expensive the next year, until eventually you are unable to keep the tradition going. It is better for each event to be high in imaginative rather than purely financial input.

Rather than spending out on private planes and five-star hotel rooms in order to take your targets to a major motor-racing event, for instance, it might be more imaginative to set up an activity day where they can all drive dune buggies across rough terrain somewhere closer to home. Likewise, it might be better to organise a cleverly themed event on your home territory rather than heading for a prestige event on the other side of the country.

To avoid the trap of having to top your previous performance each year, you need to have a long-term strategy. That means knowing, at least roughly, what you plan to do in the way of corporate entertainment for at least the next two or three, and preferably the next five years. So you need to know how it will fit in with your other marketing plans, what priority it will be receiving if business goes dramatically up, and what you could afford to do if business went down. If you set a precedent for lavish entertainment and suddenly find that you can't afford it one year due to a downturn in business, you are going to be sending exactly the wrong signals to your targets. Not only will you be letting them know that you are having tough times – which they may know anyway – but you will also be demonstrating that you were squandering money you couldn't afford on previous occasions. If, however, they see that even during the bad times your company is sufficiently strong and forward-thinking to have budgeted for a downturn, and sufficiently optimistic to continue marketing aggressively, they will be impressed and their confidence in you will be retained.

Corporate entertainment is an easy thing to cut when money is short, and internally no one will be that upset. It is easier than laying people off or cutting pay; easier even than cutting advertising budgets. The point of using this marketing tool, however, is to get the right messages about your company to the right people, and a cancelled event will do the exact opposite. So you need to choose an activity that is sustainable over the period for which you plan to use it.

In most companies no one is solely responsible for corporate entertainment; it is just tacked on to someone's list of duties. The temptation, therefore, is to go for the option requiring the least effort and input. However, this is a terrible waste of opportunity. As we will see in Chapter 8, there are plenty of professionals who can help with the planning and organisation, and more effort spent getting the concept right at the beginning will lead to far better results, and probably to cost-savings as well.

According to Simon Morris:

> Some clients will choose to go to a particular event simply because they know their competitors will be buying space and they can't afford not to be seen to be there. That can continue to work for a certain time, but eventually the costs really have to be looked at carefully. When BMW, for example, decided to be the only major motor manufacturer to pull out of the Motor Show in Britain, they were taking a calculated risk, but they had done their costings and decided that they simply couldn't justify spending such a large chunk of their marketing budget in that way. They had other priorities, dictated by their own marketing plans. If you do something because everyone else is doing it, you are putting the control of your marketing strategy into the hands of other people – your competitors – which can't be a good idea.
>
> Sometimes, however, a company will choose a style of corporate entertainment simply because they want to upstage their competition, which may be a valid marketing tactic. When ICI Films, for instance, decided to use corporate entertaining as part of their marketing mix, they were looking for ways to reach a customer base of only around 2,000 people worldwide. Those people would be subjected to approaches from competing companies all the time, so one of ICI's criteria in choosing what to do was to be better than everyone else.
>
> They also had a sponsorship deal worth millions with a Formula One racing team, designed to promote their logo all

over the world, and so they chose to link much of their corporate entertainment to the motor races.

There is a cliché within the corporate entertainment business that too many clients choose their event because it is the chairman's hobby.

Simon Morris again:

It does happen that a company will arrange a golf day because the chairman likes golf, and provided that the rest of the structure is effective it might still work. There are times, however, when the choice of event is so patently unsuitable that the client has to be talked out of it in order to avoid a disaster. We had one client who was certain that he wanted to entertain his clients with a go-karting event. Since most of them were rather portly men in their fifties, working in the drinks trade, it was obviously unsuitable. We had, therefore to find something that would be an acceptable alternative and we arranged a day with a driving expert to show the guests things they could do with ordinary cars, such as handbrake turns. That gave the day an element of self-improvement as well as being fun, and preserved the dignity of the guests.

Eddie Hoare agrees:

It is important to match the event to the guests, and that can mean the venue as well. A grand hotel that is the ultimate incentive for one person might be very intimidating to another. Some events that sound marvellous can make people feel bad. Royal Ascot, for instance, is one of the standard events in the British corporate entertainment calendar, but when a high-street jeweller insisted that I arrange a day out there for his sales people, they hated it. I warned him they would, but he said it didn't matter; they had said they wanted to go and that had provided the incentive to make them work. I feel that he should have taken account of the fact that they would not have a good time on the day. The problem at Ascot is that virtually no corporate clients can ever get into the Royal Enclosure, which immediately makes the guests feel like second-class citizens. That is exactly what they should not be made to feel like.

Elegant Days also arranges dinners at the top table of an old Oxford college, complete with all the silver and a smattering of learned fellows. Eddie Hoare explains:

> There are people who do not understand why they should eat a £100 meal sitting on wooden benches on cracked wooden floors. But the idea works wonderfully for people who perhaps went to Oxbridge colleges years ago, or who didn't go and are interested to see what it is like.
>
> You can hold events in museums or art galleries, or on boats – which are good if you want a captive audience – or anywhere else, but the people must feel both comfortable and excited by the venue, which is a difficult balance to achieve.

Chapter Summary

- Involve the guests in as little travel as possible, while making the location as exciting as possible.
- Always negotiate the prices, and look for ways to add value.
- Arrange an event well in advance and choose a time that will appeal to the guests and fit into your business plan.
- Don't stretch an event any longer than it merits.
- Inviting partners always adds value to an event.
- It is always better to reach a few people effectively than a lot of people less effectively.
- Imagination and creativity are more important than cost.
- Have a long-term strategy and fit each event into it.
- Make your guests feel comfortable and excited at the same time.

Chapter 7

Making It Work on the Day

'If corporate hospitality doesn't work for you it's because you haven't done it right,'

Philippa Bovey, PJ Promotional Services and Advantage Hospitality

The golden rule that applies throughout the planning of a corporate entertainment event but is particularly important on the day itself is 'Pay Attention to Detail'. As with so many things, the small touches make all the difference, and show that someone has taken trouble, which makes a guest feel wanted.

This principle applies in any situation. If, for instance, you are away from home on business and you walk into a bare, anonymous hotel room on a grey evening, with nothing to look forward to but a meal alone and then the television for company, you could be forgiven for feeling a twinge of depression, and you are unlikely to go away with any particularly warm feelings about the hotel, even if the accommodation and service are completely adequate.

Suppose, however, there were flowers in the room, or some fresh fruit; suppose the receptionist gave the impression that you were expected and told you something about the room you were in; suppose there was a personal note from the manager welcoming you to the hotel, and telling you what time dinner was being served; suppose when you got downstairs the waiters knew your name and took you to a table specially reserved for you . . .

All these things, even if you know they are done in the cynical cause of customer care, make your stay more pleasant, and in lifting your spirits just a little, they encourage you to come back to the same hotel again when you are next in the area.

It is the same customer care psychology, taken one step further, that makes all the difference to a corporate entertainment event.

'Host companies must look for opportunities to provide optional extras,' says Philippa Bovey. 'It might mean a gift for the ladies, hotel accommodation or transfers, a birthday cake or special diets. None of these things is difficult to arrange, provided that you anticipate them far enough in advance.'

On average between 5 and 10 per cent of people at an event will have special diet requirements, covering anything from an allergy to religious dictates or a simple dislike, and any one of them could be made to feel resentful if their needs are overlooked, so that they miss a meal or have to wait self-consciously while something is prepared for them. Nor is simply labelling someone 'vegetarian' enough; you have to be precise. Do they eat fish, eggs or dairy products, for instance? You also need to check the ingredients with care: some vegetable soup is made with beef stock for instance, and Beef Wellington can be made with pork pâté.

Chas Wheeler says he is amazed at most purchasers of corporate entertainment's lack of research. 'Whereas they should want to know everything about the product they are buying, many of them are happy to choose on the strength of a colour brochure or a telephone call from a sales person.'

The aim of the day is to make the guests feel special, with everything as pleasant and comfortable for them as possible, showing that their presence was wanted and that things have been arranged to give them an exciting and memorable day.

The Right Personnel

An event has to start with the right people there on the ground in the host camp. In many cases arrangements are left to the sales team and to hired waiters and waitresses. Guests turn up at the appointed time and follow signs to the appropriate place. When they enter they may be confronted with a group of people – perhaps from the host company, perhaps other guests – already standing around talking to one another. They may be shy and, if they don't know any of the faces already there, they will not feel able to go up and introduce themselves. They will grab a drink, if one is offered by the catering staff, and will then stand there until eventually someone else, equally lost and alone, befriends them.

No one would treat visitors to their own home in such a way, and yet they think nothing of behaving like this at a company event. A guest at a corporate event must be treated just as if he or she had arrived at the host's house. To start with a host should certainly make sure they are at the venue before the guests arrive – a guest who gets there early must not be made to feel awkward; they have in fact provided the host with an ideal opportunity to get to know them better and to start the ball rolling. If the first guests are thoroughly briefed on what is going on, they will be able to help brief other people informally as the event goes along. This will make them feel like insiders rather than outsiders – a good feeling for anyone.

It is important, therefore, that everyone on the host team knows exactly what their role in the proceedings is going to be. Someone who is already familiar with all the guests must be there, at the door, to catch them before they have a moment to feel left out. It may be that no one person fulfils that role, in which case there should be as many people there as necessary. The guests must be met and greeted by name the moment they come in. If they are being given name badges, that must happen immediately to ensure than no one has to be asked their name during the event. Hosts should also wear their badges at all times so that everyone knows who they are and can go to them with questions if necessary.

In an ideal situation they will then be introduced to the most senior person present from the host company (presuming they don't already know one another). The more senior the management attending the event, the better the results will be. Let's assume that the chief executive is the one who is there – we'll call him or her the 'lead host'. Before arriving, in fact before the guest list is even finalised, the lead host must find out who everyone is, and memorise at least something about them.

If one of the guests spends a million a year with the company, the lead host must be apprised of that fact. If someone is a new customer, or an old customer, or a dissatisfied one, they should know about it. If possible they should know some personal details in order to help the conversation. If someone has recently been divorced or bereaved, for instance, it would be useful to know that fact, so as to avoid the topic.

All the representatives from the host company should be furnished in advance with dossiers on each of the guests, containing as much information as possible about them. This will help with the planning of the day – details such as the fact that people are vegetarian or teetotal, for instance, can make a big difference to how they are treated – and with the small talk that is unavoidable at the beginning of any social gathering.

A conversation can start with something as trivial as a discussion about the journey people have had getting there, and it will go better if the host shows that he or she knows where the guests live and have come from.

For guests to be introduced to the lead host will reinforce the feeling that the company genuinely values them and wants their presence. Just as you would welcome someone to your house, the lead host must let guests know how welcome they are, demonstrating an awareness of who they are and why they have been invited.

If there are a large number of guests and the lead host is very senior, there will be time pressure if they are to meet and greet everyone. There must, therefore, be other members of the host team around the lead host, ready to take over one guest when another arrives. The lead host can then introduce the guest to the next person, who can take them off into the group.

In an ideal situation it might be that they are handed back to the person who first greeted them, the one they already know, but that person may have moved on to someone else by then. Therefore, there need to be enough people from the host company to ensure that there is always someone to spend time talking to each guest individually for a few minutes, explaining what is going to happen, introducing them to a few of the other guests, and making sure they have whatever they want.

This is not a job that can be left to the most junior people from a host company. Putting people at their ease and introducing strangers is a highly skilled and difficult job; not everyone can do it. A lot of companies think that it will be enough to hire a few pretty hostesses or ask some secretaries to fill the role, but that won't be enough.

The team from the host company should be at least equal in rank to the guests, and possibly senior to them. They shouldn't be so senior that the guests feel inhibited – it would be a mistake to closet some middle-management buyers with the chairman of a multinational corporation for too long – but they should certainly be senior enough for the guests to be flattered by their attentions, and pleased to be spending time with them. They have not found a slot in their busy schedules to come and talk to a junior member of the public relations department or the financial director's personal assistant.

It also makes sense for the host company to ensure that they have senior, competent people present because, as they are the ones who know the aims of the event, they will be able to ask the right questions and give the right answers to the guests. Nothing gives a worse impression to a guest than talking to a member of the host team and discovering that they know less about their company or less about the event than the guest does.

The host company is hoping to build personal relationships that will be useful in the ongoing business relationships they have with their guests. Some of the junior people who will actually be dealing with guests on a day-to-day basis when they get back to work should be present as well, but they must not be left to manage the whole event themselves. They can be introduced to the guest, if not already known to them, so that they can lay the foundations for what will hopefully grow into a long-term working relationship, but they must be supervised by someone senior who can ensure that the conversations go in the right direction, the guests do not become bored and the junior hosts do not suffer from attacks of shyness or verbal diarrhoea.

If you use a consultant or agent to help with the organisation of an event, part of their service will be to provide people on the day. The Cavendish consultancy, for instance, will provide a manager and a hostess, no matter how small the number of guests. They will then provide another hostess for every three tables of guests (with an average of ten people per table).

These people should not only be able to deal with all the practical details, like making sure that the drink doesn't run out and helping guests to find facilities they need, but they can also work at a social level, making small talk, introducing guests to the hosts and so on.

Well-trained and experienced staff of this sort are extremely valuable, and may be the single best reason for hiring an agency, particularly if senior members of the host team are not good at small talk. You should ensure that experienced ground staff are included in any package you are sold by an agency.

It will also be helpful to meet them beforehand, so that you can get to know them and they can ascertain your aims for the day, and be briefed about the guests. The more the agency people appear part of the host team, the more comfortable the guests will feel.

Chas Wheeler says:

I have been to so many events where the sales people from the host company, who should be looking after the guests, are just talking among themselves. They seem to think that the day has been arranged for their entertainment, not that of the guests. If they are properly briefed, that doesn't happen. They should be as well drilled as they would be if attending a major trade exhibition, where they wouldn't dream of standing around, ignoring potential and existing customers who come on to the stand.

And Philippa Bovey finds:

Being a good host or hostess at a corporate event is an innate ability. They need to have an understanding of marketing as well as operational skills, social savvy and enough numeracy to be able to deal with budgets. It is a more complex job than purely social entertaining, which is why so many companies need the help of professionals.

And Chas Wheeler again:

There should ideally be two sales people sitting on each table, and each of them should be armed with a fact sheet in advance to help them with conversation. A lot of people find hosting for a few hours very difficult, and so they must be given enough back-up training and material to ensure that they don't dry up.

It is better to have a sit-down meal than a buffet. If you have paid that much for a meal, I don't think you should have to get up and queue, and it can break up conversations. The way most buffets are arranged they are usually terribly slow. It comes back to the idea of providing the same standards as a first-class restaurant or hotel.

Making Enough Space

Chas Wheeler outlines his approach:

> I always prepare a floorplan of the marquee or room in advance. I believe it is important to give people as much space as possible. The average space per person in a standard package is 15 square feet. I believe 25 square feet is better. I also prefer to put eight people on to tables designed for ten – again, it gives more room and makes people feel more comfortable. If you allow for that extra space, you can then include a sitting or reception area with sofas and chairs which will completely change the atmosphere of the room. If you buy a standard package, you will probably get only the tables and dining chairs, and for the rest of the time people will be standing uncomfortably around. It doesn't cost much more to hire some extra furniture, as long as you know where to go, which is where it helps to have an experienced agent or consultant on your side.

Looking After Guests

From the moment they are invited to the moment they leave the event, guests must feel that they are being looked after. Not only should the host team be there before the guests; they must also leave after them. If on the day a guest doesn't like the food being served at lunch, they must know who to tell, and that person must be empowered to find alternatives. If they are concerned about where they parked their car, or how they are going to get home at the end of the day, someone must be there with the time and the ability to sort out the problems without fuss.

This level of care has to start before guests arrive. You must make sure that they know how to get to the venue, have been given maps if necessary and somewhere special to park, together with contact telephone numbers for any emergency. They must be approached personally a day or two before by someone who is going to be there to find out if they have any worries. If at the last minute guests are still concerned about travel arrangements, or they can't make it under their own steam, then someone must go and fetch them.

If you have decided that you want someone as your guest, then you must do everything in your power to make sure that they are able to come and that they enjoy themselves once there.

On the whole, this means providing them with clear, concise information at all stages of the operation. People feel really comfortable only when they know what is going on; everyone becomes anxious when confronted with the unknown. If there is going to be a sit-down meal, for instance, they will want to know where they should sit. You will have decided in advance how you want to arrange things, either with formal place cards or with people helping themselves and sitting wherever they want. It doesn't matter what you decide to do as long as it serves the purposes of the day, and as long as everyone knows what is expected of them.

Guests must also be told of any special clothes and/or equipment they will need to bring. If there is any danger that they might come with the wrong items, make sure you have a supply of things to lend them – boots, waterproof clothing, umbrellas, warm jumpers or whatever.

According to Simon Morris:

An alarmingly large percentage of host companies never get the details right. Most often they fail to give their guests sufficient information. They may give them no directions, or they get them to a major venue and then fail to tell them which gate to go through, so they end up walking miles. If an organiser has visited the venue only when it is an open field, it is hard to visualise just how difficult it will be to get around once the tents have been erected and the crowds have arrived.

It often helps to let guests have some details of the traditions and etiquettes of the event, so that they do not feel awkward or out of place, and many organisers miss obvious opportunities to make the event special, like the erection of banners or getting their guests mentioned on the commentary. At most large events a commentator is very accessible, sitting in a tower somewhere with nothing much to talk about most of the time. Organisers can very easily introduce themselves and explain what they are doing there and ask for the guests to be welcomed over the loudspeakers. It is surprising how much difference a touch like this will make to a guest.

Chas Wheeler agrees:

You can't do too much for guests. Because they are on a day out they have usually switched off, which means they don't want to have to think too hard about where to go or what to do. They want to be looked after. It is always worth checking at the last moment with the local police and the venue to make sure nothing has changed. It is no good preparing maps and then finding that the organisers have moved the entrances round at the last moment because of road works. If they need special badges, you must make sure they receive them in advance, but also have some spares there on the day, because some of them will have left theirs at home.

In an ideal situation an organiser will visit a venue a year before (if it is a regular event) to see how it runs.
Simon Morris again:

It may be that the actual competitions won't start till ten in the morning, but if you tell your guests to arrive at ten they will spend an hour and a half sitting in traffic jams trying to get through the gates. The organisers at the venue may not warn you of this, simply because they never attend the event as customers. A host or consultant who has experienced it, however, can make alternative arrangements. You might, for instance, invite them to come at eight o'clock for breakfast and then take them to walk the course, visit the stables or pits, or simply explore the event.

By reconnoitring the event the year before you can familiarise yourself with details like where the toilets are, and medical tents, and all the other things that make the difference between order and chaos on the day. It is also worth having copies of the previous year's programmes and ground plans, to help to understand how the event works.

It is always worth meeting the officials at the venue a few months beforehand and getting to know them, so that any problems on the day can be sorted out quickly and they know who you are. It also helps to have a senior name to drop if you have trouble with a steward or some other junior official.

The Weather

In most countries the weather is unpredictable. Whatever you organise you must have alternative arrangements for the eventuality of pouring rain, strong winds, dust storms or whatever else is typical to the area. You must also make the guests aware that, whatever the weather is like, the event will continue; otherwise they may wake up in the morning, see it is pouring with rain and assume that everything's off. Assure them that the event will be going ahead come what may. Once you have laid all your plans, it is vital that everyone attends; even a few absentees could leave a sad gap in a carefully organised group.

Provided that you have made efforts to keep them entertained, guests will forgive you for elements beyond your control. If they don't come at all, you have simply lost your marketing opportunity and wasted your time and money.

If, for instance, you have invited everyone to watch a championship tennis match and rain stops play all day, you must make sure that there are alternative arrangements indoors. The meal must go ahead uninterrupted in the hospitality tent, someone should be there to entertain the guests and whatever happens they should go home at the end of the day feeling that their hosts did the best they could and that an enjoyable and useful time was had by all, even if no one got to see any tennis.

If you are organising an activity day yourselves, then make sure that the chance of extremes of weather are part of the fun. If you are taking guests out to drive some splendid four-wheel-drive vehicles, then wet conditions will make the going all the more exciting.

If arduous conditions are an obvious part of the fun, and everyone expects to come home muddy, then no one will complain. It is important, however, that all the elements under your control are made as favourable as possible. During the time that your guests are sitting inside, for instance, they must be kept at a good temperature. That means providing heating or air-conditioning if either are likely to be necessary, or shading people from the sun and strong winds. If they are outside, then they must be given shelter where it is possible, umbrellas and waterproofs if it is raining and sun hats if the heat is uncomfortable.

When the Profile Partnership was organising a celebrity cricket match at a hotel, they took the precaution of booking the newly built ballroom as well as the outdoor cricket pitch. On the day it poured with rain, so they merely moved the match indoors and used a soft ball. The added novelty value made the day so memorable that they have since put indoor cricket on the list of regular options they suggest to new clients.

According to Chas Wheeler:

> If there is any danger of the weather causing an interruption, I always make sure there are plenty of games in the marquee, and videos. I might even set up some casino tables if that is appropriate, perhaps with bottles of champagne as prizes. One client I had used to book the same day at Wimbledon every year, and it always seemed to rain, but he liked it that way because he said it meant people stayed in the marquee and talked rather than wasting time watching the tennis.

Free Gifts

For obvious reasons, then, umbrellas and sun visors have become the standard gifts for hosts to give to guests at corporate entertainment events.

Guests do not have to go away with gifts, and having nothing is better than having something inappropriate or cheap-looking. If you do decide to give mementoes, it will be worth including items relevant to the theme of the day. It could be a statuette commemorating their feats during an activity day, or a brace of pheasants from a shoot they've been on. It doesn't matter what it is, as long as it is going to enhance the impression you have been trying to create from the beginning.

There is no point giving printed T-shirts unless guests are going to wear them on the day for a special reason; there is no point giving pens with the company logo on unless they are needed during the day for filling out something like race cards. When ICI organised a day watching cross-country riding at Gatcombe Park, for instance, they did a deal with Barbour, makers of prestige waterproof countrywear, to supply jackets.

The most appropriate gift might be a framed photograph of the guest at the event, or a certificate to say that they have taken part in the activity.

The Right Amount of Corporate Theming

Too much corporate theming of an event will detract from the social aspect and make it seem overly commercial; too little may mean that you are missing opportunities to imprint the name of your company on the memories of important target audiences.

One of the aims of an event is to give the right impression of the company to the guests. That means that you want to show you are confident and efficient, not that you are brash and hard-selling. Having well-printed signposts to the venue with the company logo on, and similarly perso-nalised equipment, will add to the feeling that the day is well organised. Huge banners and piles of company brochures will give the impression that everyone has been brought there to be sold to.

Some companies will go to the most extravagant lengths to ensure that everything they do reflects the corporate logo. Flower arrangements will be in the company colours and carpets will be woven with the company initials, glasses will be engraved and napkins will be embroidered. There may be a place for such rigid theming, and it may be a necessary discipline in some large companies where a mix of styles could be confusing to a customer, but it may also be unnecessary in a corporate entertainment environment, where people need to be made to feel comfortable before anything else.

Details of Decor

Whether or not they are themed to the company logo, flowers are often important for making a hospitality tent or hotel conference room look more attractive. It is also important to decide whether you want people to sit or stand. If you are hoping that people are going to sit in small groups at times of the day when nothing else is happening, so that they can talk business, then you must ensure that there are comfortable sofas and chairs in the most suitable groupings.

If there is a danger of long periods during which nothing much is happening, then you must arrange suitable distractions for the guests. These might be games, television sets or simply piles of magazines likely to appeal to the people in question.

Again, as with guests in your own home, you don't want them to feel they have to stand up and make formal conversation if they would rather sit down and relax.

At formally laid tables you should leave people plenty of elbow room, so that they are completely comfortable. Chairs with arms and personalised menu cards are details that make people feel good, and cost very little extra to provide.

Personalised Printing

Anything to do with the day that requires printing work should be done to the highest possible standard, and personalised to the individual guest wherever possible. This can apply to a wallet of instructions on how to get there and details of what will happen, menus, score cards and anything else that is needed. In these days of laser printing, it costs no more to personalise things but makes an enormous difference to the recipients.

'It is surprising how many guests,' says Simon Morris, 'will take things like menus away with them at the end of the day as souvenirs.'

Guests at the Manila Hotel in the Philippines find when they arrive in their rooms a list of distinguished former guests. The list is about a page long, and includes names like General MacArthur and Somerset Maugham. Guests will probably scan down the list, because most of us like to think we are sharing the life-style of the rich and famous (our licence to boast again), and they will suddenly come across their own name in alphabetical order. It is the smallest of touches but will make guests laugh; it will demonstrate that although the hotel has a distinguished history it is not as grand and impersonal as they might at first have thought, and it has given them a simple, effective memento to take home. The cost? Just a few moments of somebody's time. That is imaginative attention to detail.

Getting the Guest Mix Right

Any host or hostess knows that if they get the guest mix right at a party, it will go with a swing. Conversely, if you get it wrong, you will have to work yourself into the ground trying to keep everyone happy. While the host team have to be skilled at breaking the ice and making people feel welcome and comfortable, it is then important that the guests begin to interact among themselves if the day is to work well. The hosts can't hope to carry the whole burden from start to finish.

Getting the right mix of guests must be part of the early planning stage. How successful you are will depend on how much you know about the individuals and how large a pool you have to choose from. If you have ten clients to entertain regularly, then you will need to find ways of making the day go well whether they get on with one another or not. If you have 100 potential targets, then you can begin to think about the possibilities of breaking them up into smaller groups of like-minded individuals.

Many companies find that it is useful to mix satisfied customers with potential customers, so that the former can help to spread the good news about the host company, and the latter can see the ways in which the host team interacts with their customers.

Chapter Summary

- No detail is too small for attention.
- Find out everyone's individual needs.
- Personalise everything that can be personalised.
- Have a fully briefed host team of sufficient seniority.
- Always arrive before the guests and leave after them.
- Meet and greet everyone at the door.
- Include junior operational staff from the host company, but brief and train them thoroughly and introduce them to the guests.
- Give the host team all the necessary professional back-up in the way of caterers and organisers.
- Ensure everyone has enough space by preparing a floorplan.
- Ensure guests always know what is going to be happening.
- If planning to use a major event, visit it the year before to familiarise yourself.
- Help your guests to avoid traffic jams, queues and other inconveniences.
- Get to know the officials at the organised events.
- Be prepared for bad weather.
- Get the level of corporate theming right.
- Look for ways to improve the interior decorations.
- Encourage guests to interact with one another.

Chapter 8

Who to Go to for Help

Some of the most important aspects of the work involved in corporate entertaining have to be done in-house – there is simply no alternative. The collection of information on target guests, for instance, can be done only by those who know what they are looking for and have access to the people themselves. The decisions regarding the long-term aims of the campaign also have to be made by the marketing department and other senior managers who are privy to the company's overall strategies, know what budgets are likely to be available and know the priorities within those budgets. None of this can be effectively done by outside advisers.

Once these basic strategic decisions have been made, however, it is then possible to bring in a range of experts who can both help with creative and imaginative ideas based on a specialist knowledge of the marketplace and take on some of the donkey work involved in getting the event up and running.

Some of the world's largest companies now have whole departments set up to handle nothing but corporate entertainment, with annual budgets running into millions. But these departments will still use the services of specialised consultants, just as a marketing department will use the services of advertising and sales promotion agencies, public relations consultants and all the other specialist management experts, and just as a financial department will hire outside accountants and auditors. There is simply too much information for any one company to be able to keep abreast of it all themselves – too many new venues, new services, new ideas. Only by listening to a variety of specialists can buyers of corporate entertainment services hope to find out what is available. Without this market knowledge there is a danger that they will simply keep doing what they have done before, thus missing opportunities and failing to keep up with competitors.

The Novelty Factor

Novelty is always important in the corporate entertainment industry because it is one of the major 'hooks' with which to attract the attention of targets. People want to experience things before everyone else does, they want to be able to talk about things their friends and neighbours haven't yet had the opportunity to try. Something that was a new idea a couple of years ago will be old hat by now – first it was tennis matches and motor-racing, then came clay-pigeon shooting and trying out four-wheel-drive vehicles, and so on. While all these things continue to have their place in the market, companies that use entertainment regularly have to have a constant supply of new ideas. They must know what the options are, and what their competitors are doing, in order to stay ahead of the field and provide their targets with real reasons for accepting invitations. This sort of information is most easily found from consultants.

Consultants and Agents

There is no shortage of people who call themselves consultants in corporate entertainment, and claim to be able to hold the client's hand from start to finish. There is a limit, however, to those who can actually do so effectively.

Some of them are selling packages to major spectator

events and will supply 'consultancy' services to their customers to add value to the packages. They are still, however, selling a particular product and so are not completely objective in their advice. Others are non-specialists, working in related areas like public relations or catering, who make corporate entertainment part of their service. How good they are will depend entirely on the calibre of the individuals involved and the previous experience they have had.

As Philippa Bovey says:

> Unless an agent is adding value, there is no reason to use them. Often they are simply buying packages from other people and marking them up, in which case the client would do as well to go direct to the organisers of the packages. We are happy to act as brokers in this way if that is what the client wants, but in most cases they want us to tweak the packages to give them added value, which might mean colour coordinating the marquee, changing some horrible chairs for nicer ones, or adding flowers and canapés. In some cases the agents have their own events that they have been appointed to handle; then they may be the best people to deal with in any situation.

Eddie Hoare has made a conscious decision:

> We deliberately don't have packages. We go to our clients with a blank sheet of paper and ask them what it is they want to achieve. The market seems to divide up into the sophisticated companies, who have used corporate entertainment a great deal and know exactly what they want – such as the fast-moving consumer-goods companies, the motor industry, financial services and pharmaceuticals – and the newcomers, who want guidance on where to start.

There is a growing number of specialist organisations setting out to supply corporate entertainment as a marketing tool, in exactly the way that has been described. Their problem historically is that many potential clients for corporate entertainment have had bad experiences in the past with people who are little more than ticket-brokers, or even outright con-men. Being a young and immature industry, corporate entertainment has had more than its fair share of cowboy operators and it has been hard work for the reputable consultants to fight against the resulting poor image.

Because of these uncertainties, it is important that a client company does not hand over the whole responsibility for an event to someone they have never worked with before. Every detail must be checked, in advance, by someone in-house. Once you have worked a few times with a consultant, and have found them to be reliable, you can begin to relinquish some of the responsibility, but never all of it. Remember, it is the client company that is inviting the guests, not the consultant. If the host's personal stamp is missing, it will show; the event will look like nothing more than a package bought off the shelf.

Think of the difference between a house decorated from top to bottom by an interior decorator, with no reference to the personal taste and preferences of the owner, and a house decorated by professionals following the instructions of the owner. The owner may ask the advice of the professionals, and will rely on them to get the job done on time and to brief, but the final effect is the one that they were striving to achieve, not the one they bought and are living with as if in a luxury hotel.

According to Chas Wheeler:

> A lot of client companies tend to think that they can do it all themselves, and perhaps with a bit of practice and enough time they could, but how many of them have that experience or the time? Most of the ones who try to do it themselves end up with half-full marquees. The really successful companies know exactly when to subcontract.

The secret of a successful relationship with a corporate entertainment consultant, as with any other sort of consultant, lies in the personal rapport between the people involved. If you like and trust someone, and find that you understand one another, then the chances are that you will work well together. Consultants vary in tastes and abilities, just as clients do; while one will be particularly good at organising discreet little gatherings for wine-tastings and nights at the opera, another will be better at taking large crowds to football matches and overseeing huge gala dinners. It may be that you would prefer to build a relationship with just one and then let them handle everything, but you might equally well use different ones in each specialist sector.

It is more important to hire a company whose staff you like, trust and respect than one that handles the most events or is the most famous. The success of any corporate entertainment event will rest on the relationships between the people involved, not the name of the consultancy (although you are more likely to trust and respect someone with a good track record).

All too often in the past inexperienced buyers of corporate entertainment services have been sold products – sometimes over the phone – that neither fit in with their long-term plans, nor live up to the promises made for them. The goals must be decided first, and then objective consultants can be called in to give their advice. The ones who are seriously developing the market all have good track records and will be able to supply lists of satisfied clients for a prospective customer to check credentials.

You need to establish track records to find out consultants' experience in handling businesses like yours, and their experience at the venue you have chosen. One of the main reasons to hire an agent is that they should have more experience than you. Do they have sufficient staff to handle every event, and how many of them will be looking after your guests? What do their offices look like? You need to meet the senior personnel as well as the people who will be there on the day. Find out whether they are providing official facilities and what their ticket sources are, and ask for every detail of the package they are selling. How personalised can they make the event, and how visible will your corporate image be? Can they help with special requirements outside the standard package? The more questions you ask at the beginning, the fewer nasty surprises you will get later on.

Once you have found someone you like, you should involve them in the decision-making process as early as possible. The clearer the idea they have of your aims, and the better they understand the profiles of your targets, the better they will able to tailor an event to suit them. By being involved in the planning stages they can help with suggestions as to the alternatives that might be suitable, and can assist in the putting together of costings on various different options. At the early stages you are using them for their ability to produce new ideas for you to consider. In many cases they will not even charge for this part of the service and will give you a price for the whole package once it has been finalised; or they will charge set fees for their organisational services.

It is in the second, organisational, phase that a good consultant really begins to be of value, saving executive time by undertaking all the tedious chores involved in making the event happen, and hopefully saving money with their buying experience. They can help with the design of the invitations and advise on the best ways to tempt targets to accept. They can liaise with the venue, the caterers, the transport-providers, the flower-arrangers, the printers and anyone else who might be involved, from a celebrity speaker to a supplier of personalised balloons.

They may also save a client money by knowing how to negotiate with venues and suppliers, and being able to haggle from positions of strength due to their greater knowledge of the marketplace. Sometimes it is possible to do deals with suppliers, such as a champagne house that is keen to get its products used at certain types of event and so will supply things like back-up staff and promotional and point-of-sale material free of charge.

The client and consultant must work as a team, and the client must give their personal stamp of approval to all the decisions taken. Someone from the client side, for instance, must visit the venue in advance and talk to the caterers about the menu; they must actually see what the room or tent is going to look like and know exactly how it will be furnished. While a good consultant can be relied on to get the logistics right, only the client themselves can ensure that the 'feel' is appropriate for their guests. And when attention to detail is so important, it is better to have two sets of people checking everything than one.

Once you have found a consultant you like, then you can integrate them into your team. They could actually be important members of the host team on the day. They could act as staff members of the host company as far as the guests are concerned, making sure everything is running smoothly and that neither the host team nor the guest team has to worry about any of the practicalities on the day, leaving them free to both enjoy themselves and work at the main objective of the day, which is to build relationships. A host who is having to rush around discovering why the champagne isn't chilled, or why there aren't enough chairs, is not going to be in a sufficiently calm frame of mind to concentrate on talking with the guests and finding out more about them.

Peter Selby of Keith Prowse Hospitality, which is the official supplier of corporate entertainment facilities at most of the major British sporting events, is predictably sceptical about the advantages of using consultants.

> If you've decided what you want to do, you might as well buy it direct from the event organisers. If, on the other hand, you have a budget that you want to invest in corporate enter-tainment, then there are any number of people who will be willing to advise you on how to do it. You must remember, however, that they all have vested interests of some sort, just like insurance brokers.
>
> There are also people who have set themselves up to be

purely hospitality brokers. They will just act as the middlemen and make no claims to do any more than that, and they too have a niche in the market.

Beware

In the past unscrupulous operators have found a number of ways of getting extra money from customers. They might, for instance, tell you that the package is all-inclusive but then, nearer the day, they will send you a 'special menu' with an option to upgrade. Because the special menu doesn't look that good, you panic at the thought of how bad the ordinary one must be and so pay up.

Alternatively, you may suddenly realise that you have bought enough parking space for only one space per four guests. Since most of them will be coming on their own or in pairs, you panic again but when you ask for more spaces you find the cost is enormous. You may also find that things like the services of a barman are not included in the package.

The need to check every detail yourself unless you know the agent personally is borne out by any number of cases. For example, a client was told there would be a 'glass-fronted box' and arrived only to find that the box didn't even face the event. Others were offered boxes that turned out to be a mile or more away from the main event. Make sure that if the hospitality village is outside the turnstiles of the event, readmission will not be a problem. You do not want to find your guests going back to the tent for tea and then being unable to return to the grounds.

In some cases organisers have been known to offer 'free champagne' for bookings above a certain number. The client, thinking they will be able to use it at the event, thus saving money, discovers on the day that the 'free' bottles are going to be given to them afterwards, while bottles bought on the day cost way above the recommended price.

While the industry is doing its best to stamp out sharp practice of this sort, there are always going to be unscrupulous organisations cashing in on innocent customers. The rules are to take up references, meet the people you are going to be dealing with and visit and talk to the venue as well. Find a consultant who wants to form a long-term relationship with you, not simply sell you as much as possible.

Buying Packages

There are companies providing ready-made corporate entertainment packages. A number of them even have a standard set of themed party ideas – variations on the toga party idea that was so popular in the early days of corporate entertainment. These packages are professionally thought out and produced, and provide just what they promise. What they don't have, however, is the personal touch, and it is up to the client, or the client's consultant, to add those to anything they might buy 'off the shelf'.

If, for instance, you buy a package at one of the major sporting events that includes a tent and a standard catering service, this may well be all you get. When your guests arrive, they will find that yours is just one of the many identical tents in a hospitality village, with standard tables, standard chairs and food that looks just as you would expect. This package may suit your needs exactly, but the chances are that with a minimum of extra effort – a few extra pieces of furniture, a change in the menu, the inclusion of some live music or the laying of a nicer carpet – a standard tent could be transformed into something special. Such details are easily taken care of and might make the difference between an ordinary day and a special one.

As Jim Bignall of Cavendish says:

> If you hire an agency, they will make sure nothing slips through the net. It may be that a package bought direct from

the venue, for instance, is sub-standard. We always arrive at the event the day before and quite often we are having to replace floor boards or mend leaks in the roof, and we then add all the extra touches like pictures on the walls and table centres. A good agency can create an atmosphere and a buzz which may well be completely missing otherwise.

Starting with the Venue

It may be that preliminary research into your target group and your goals makes choice of venue your first priority, before you have found a consultant or a supplier of packages.

If so, then the venue you decide on would be the best place to start making inquiries. Most of the major sporting and cultural events will have one or two official providers of corporate entertainment services, and may be able to recommend a few more consultants whom they know to be reputable. If you hire a consultant at random, you run the risk of discovering later that they have no official recognition at your chosen venue, and you will end up with a second-rate service and possibly also have to pay more than you would for a first-rate service from a recognised consultant. You may even discover, as has happended in the past, that the entry tickets you have been sold are forgeries. It is hard to imagine a more embarrassing situation than having to tell 100 of your best customers that they can't get into the event you have invited them to because their tickets aren't valid.

It is important that someone from the host company goes down to the venue to see what is on offer. What sounds wonderful in a brochure might be a great disappointment in reality. A tent described as being 'only a few yards' from the track might in fact have another tent in between. A tented village described as being 'a few minutes' walk' from a stadium might be the other side of a six-lane motorway. A host company will be investing a great deal in an event, and it would be tragic to ruin the occasion by failing to check everything in advance.

At the more sophisticated venues there are teams of people dedicated to working with companies that want to provide corporate entertainment. Like the package-providers, however, they are supplying a standard service and any add-on value will have to be negotiated for by the client.

If you decide to dispense with the services of a consultant and handle everything in-house, there are still a number of service suppliers who will make your life a great deal easier if you allow them to.

Caterers

Very few companies will undertake their own catering, although it can provide an extremely effective personal touch if they do. One public relations company in London liked to take their clients to Henley each year, and organised every detail themselves, right down to making the food and buying the drink to go into their picnic hampers. Not only were they able to build their relationships with their clients, but they were also able to show off their skills at organising an event and to make it truly personal – presumably saving money at the same time.

Most organisers, however, will hire professional caterers. They come in all shapes and sizes. If you want to make catering part of the bait, then you will need to use a named chef or restaurant. In Britain, for instance, names like the Roux Brothers and Pru Leith can add an extra dimension to the day, giving targets an idea of what they can expect. If you are going to be using a restaurant, then in Europe a Michelin star will make all the difference to the number of acceptances you get to your invitation to a gourmet meal.

Most of the well-known catering companies are experienced in providing meals at different venues. Some venues insist on their own caterers and do not allow outsiders, but they are the minority.

According to Chas Wheeler:

Catering is one of the most important aspects of an event. If you are tailor-making your own event, then you have no problems because you can serve whatever food you like. If you are going to one of the big venues, however, where they are mass-catering, the chances are the quality will be very poor, and expensive. In the past people have been willing to accept these standards, which is why things haven't improved, but no one should expect things to be this bad. If you hire an experienced agent they will be able to advise you on what the standards of catering are likely to be at any given venue, and they may be able to improve on them for you, but you have to know what is possible.

The official caterers at these events say that the organisers knock them down so far on price that they can't do anything better. An agent may be able to do something about it for you. I introduced Roux Brothers food at major events at the end of the 1980s, which meant that for the first time hosts could offer à la carte menus, and it didn't cost that much more.

This is one of the advantages of being outside an event. I ran the biggest hospitality village outside Wimbledon for a number of years, catering for 3,600 people. It was only 100 yards' walk from the event and we were able to serve whatever food we wanted.

And for Eddie Hoare:

It is always a mistake to choose caterers on price alone. What you should be looking for is an imaginative menu. Too many companies just serve up the same basic business lunch menus. Sometimes it is safer to go for one of the major companies, but a smaller company may work harder if your event is likely to be one of the biggest contracts they are going to get that year. It comes down to personalities and experience. Personally I like to use companies who hire professional waiters, not just casual labour, and who put them in smart uniforms. Liveried staff will make a big difference to the atmosphere of a meal.

Suppliers

If you are planning an activity day you will nearly always need to seek the help of professional suppliers, since only they will know where to get hold of the necessary equipment and the staff trained to work it. This is particularly true if the equipment is in any way dangerous.

Venue-Finding

One of the highly onerous tasks involved in the management of an event that can be delegated out is venue-finding. If, for instance, you have decided to organise an event for which you need a hotel or large house of a certain type within a certain radius, you could start going through every directory you can find, contacting each establishment, going to see them and haggling over details. Alternatively, you could hire someone else to do this legwork for you. It will save you time and money, and shouldn't cost you anything.

Hotel-booking and conference-placement agents have been around for some years now, but it is only recently that their business has started to boom, in line with the conference and business-travel industries. The agencies work on a commission basis, similar to that operated by the travel trade, with most hotels paying a rate of between 8 and 10 per cent on bedroom bookings and 8 per cent on accommodation and prebooked food for conferences or events. The more marketing-oriented hotels are happy to work with these agencies, understanding that they can provide business during periods of low demand or at late notice. Agencies can be particularly attractive when a venue has to fill a gap caused, say, by a cancellation.

James O'Neill, founder and general manager of Inntel, one of the leading agencies in the UK, explains:

> From the industry's point of view we function like an extra salesforce working on commission only. Most agencies maintain a basic database of hotels and venues which is updated using questionnaires sent out to new or previously unidentified establishments. Some agencies will produce their own hotel guides and some even their own conference-venue guides.

Good venue-finding agencies specialise in knowing exactly what is available where. If they don't know of something, they will go out and look for it. They will find out as much as possible about the client's requirements and will suggest a number of possibilities. They will then encourage the client to meet them on-site to inspect the short-listed venues for themselves, although they mostly find that once they have gained a client's confidence, the client will tend to trust their judgement from then on.

As O'Neill says:

> Venue-searching can be complex and frustrating. To start with you can't always believe what the hotels tell you over the phone. You have to go and see for yourself what is being offered. If, when trying to match a client's requirements, you ask a hotel if it can meet certain criteria, some will say yes even when they can't. I think they work on the premise that if they can get you to their hotel, they will be able to sell you something you don't quite want. It can be terribly frustrating, and is certainly time-consuming, especially when you have spelled out the requirements in detail in advance.

For most in-house people the finding and choosing of venues for events is an additional task on top of their own jobs. It is a tedious chore that tends to get pushed to the bottom of the list. By using a professional venue-finder you can quickly come up with a short-list of possible locations that meet your basic criteria, leaving yourself more time to deal with all the other details of the operation. For most clients the financial saving will be less valuable than the time aspect. Many of the leading agencies also have links with the major sporting and cultural events.

While a client company should always double-check everything that is promised to and done for them by any outside agency, a number of talented people exist in the marketplace to help companies put on more imaginative and effective events with less effort and sometimes less cost.

Making the Accommodation Work

If a host company decides that they want to include accom-modation in the package they are offering to guests, they need to plan it well in advance. If they are attending a major event, they may find that all the hotel space in the immediate vicinity is already taken, in which case they will have to look further afield. If you are going to have to take guests away from the venue to their accommodation, then you must make sure that something special is arranged for them at the hotel, like a dinner or a reception. It is not enough simply to take them off in a bus and drop them somewhere to sleep. There must be a reason for them to be there.

Chapter Summary

- Targeting must be done in-house.
- All final decisions must be taken by the host company, not by a sub-contractor.
- Hosts need to keep up to date with new ideas in the marketplace.
- Consultants and agents can be used for creative and imaginative ideas as well as for the donkey-work.
- Always hire individuals you like and trust rather than their companies.
- Involve consultants as early as possible in the process.
- Establish their track record – experience in the business and at the chosen event, current client list and staff numbers.
- Visit their offices and meet their senior personnel.
- Be imaginative with catering.
- If the accommodation is separate from the event, make it part of the attraction.

Chapter 9

Spectator Events

Taking guests to watch major sporting or cultural events is one of the mainstays of the corporate entertainment business, particularly the sporting side, although the arts are doing their best to catch up.

I dare say that in ancient Rome merchant princes would entertain their best customers in luxurious boxes overlooking the gladiatorial arenas. Anyone who can provide some sort of special access to a popular event has a hook with which to fish for targets.

The attractions are obvious. The major events are often high points in a country's social calendar, like the Prix de l'Arc de Triomphe in Paris or Royal Ascot in Britain, giving guests a chance to feel part of high society, perhaps even to see some of the people they normally only read about in the papers. In many cases the crowds are as interesting to watch as the events themselves, and if you can get your guests into a privileged position for 'people-spotting' – on a luxury boat during a sailing, powerboat or rowing event, for example, or in a box at an opera or ballet – they will have a day to remember, whatever the quality of the entertainment.

Events such as the Grand Prix races held in the streets of Monte Carlo, Detroit and Adelaide, and the superbowl, are often exciting and atmospheric. Others such as rare live concerts by major singing stars might be exclusive and harder to get into.

The main thing is that they provide enthusiasts with a

chance to see their heroes in action. People can watch golfing, tennis and football stars from the best possible vantage points, see crowned heads playing polo, household-name racing drivers dicing with death, and great singers and dancers giving classic performances in glamorous surroundings; and be part of the atmosphere – something that never comes across on television or film.

While most people like the idea of having ringside seats at important events, the majority of us are deterred from going by the problems involved – whether real or imagined. How will we get the tickets? How will we know if they are good ones? How will we get there? Will we have to arrive early to find good places, and then have to wait hours for the event to start? Will there be anything decent to eat or drink, or will we be queuing for hours just to get a hamburger and a Coke? Where will we park? Will we miss the last train home? Will it take hours to get out of the car park at the end? Will it be freezing cold or boiling hot? Will the lavatories be unbearable? Will we be able to see anything when we get there?

What a company invitation has to do is stress all the positive elements – the glamour, the excitement, the atmosphere – and at the same time alleviate all the fears. The host, in effect, has to be able to promise that they will get their guests to the venue in comfort, show them where to park and where to aim for, entertain them in comfortable surroundings, with whatever food and drink they want, ensure that they are in the best seats and are not kept waiting at any time, while making sure that they understand everything that is going on.

In other words hosts have got to demonstrate that they will deal with all the negative elements, leaving guests free to enjoy the event for what it is.

Taking people to watch an event seems such a relatively simple thing to do that every company involved in corporate entertainment does it at one time or another. However, popularity has served to devalue the currency, and has led to most of them doing it very ineffectively.

In the worst possible instance a supplier might let a client company have tickets to an event that are then distributed to various members of staff, who then pass the tickets on to members of their family. No doubt this giving and receiving is very pleasant for all concerned, but does anyone remember who actually paid for the tickets in the first place? Has anything at all been achieved in marketing terms?

Only one stage better is the hospitality tent that serves up a meal to guests and then allows them to come and go as they please, with no guidance or organisation. Once again, the name of the host company is unlikely to register with guests, and if any impression is left at all, it will be of a bunch of fools who handed out freebies for no apparent reason.

The Sports

Most of the major sporting events are very keen to encourage corporate hospitality in one form or another, since it provides them with a major source of revenue, often more than straight ticket sales to the general public. At the same time they don't want to let so many companies in that the atmosphere of the event – and therefore half its appeal – disappears in a sea of business invitations.

One of the most frequently heard complaints is that real fans are unable to get, or can't afford, tickets to events because the market has been inundated by rich companies with big budgets inviting guests who would rather stay in the tents talking business than actually watch what's going on. While there is a degree of truth in the accusation, good corporate hospitality should not work that way.

There are only two reasons for using a spectator sport in the first place.

- It is the thing most likely to excite your targets and make them accept an invitation.

- It is in some way relevant to your business and your company's image. A grand prix motor race, for instance, may be relevant to a company active in the motor trade.

There are a number of reasons why a spectator sport might be a bad idea.

- If it is popular, there may be other people inviting your client to the same event.
- If it is popular, there will be large crowds, and that means you immediately lose some of your ability to control the environment and what happens within your event.
- There are limits to the amount of 'tailoring' you can do to a major event.
- A spectator event that appeals to some people will turn off a number of others, whereas a tailored event can be made to fit more people's tastes.
- Spectating at some events is a relatively static pastime. Once people are in their seats, they will be talking only to the people on either side of them, and for much of the time they will be silently watching the event. A participative event, on the other hand, can be tailored to give the maximum amount of communication and interaction between the attendees, thus creating greater scope for the building of relationships.
- A spectator event takes place in one location, and this means that people may have to travel further to reach it.

All too often buyers of corporate hospitality choose to entertain at a specific sporting event because they themselves enjoy it. While that is fine, if the company can afford it, no one should be fooled into thinking that it is a marketing tool. The customers may still attend, and perhaps in some cases relationships will successfully be built, but that will be more by luck than judgement.

The Arts

Much of what has been said for sporting events also applies to the arts. It tends to be the 'high arts', such as opera and ballet, that attract corporate entertainers, because they are well regarded in social terms, the tickets can be expensive and hard to come by, and they imbue the host with a certain degree of status. But West End and Broadway shows that are hard to get into can be equally attractive to guests, and can easily be built into something larger, perhaps involving a night at a suitable hotel, a gala dinner and a business meeting or conference as well.

It is important, however, that the event is something that guests could not easily arrange for themselves. A visit to a cinema is not going to excite targets, but tickets for a gala première might well, particularly if they will be meeting the celebrities. A ticket to the opera might not excite them, but dinner in a private room at the opera house before the show, and then a chance to meet the stars afterwards, might.

Sponsorship

If an event is highly relevant to a company's image, there may well be a sponsorship angle as well. The event's organisers are often as keen to attract sponsorship money as they are to attract corporate hospitality, and many of the big events are now linked to major companies.

Part of most sponsorship deals is an agreement to provide a certain number of free tickets and access to entertainment facilities at the venues that sponsors can use for corporate hospitality.

It is always tempting to think, as these tickets are there and, to all intents and purposes, are free, that the company should make use of them rather than go to the trouble of thinking up other corporate hospitality ideas. This is rather a short-sighted view.

If, when deciding which event to sponsor, the company has made a decision partly because they know that it will fit in with their corporate hospitality plans, then the sponsorship link will be positive and will help to integrate the various marketing efforts involved.

If, however, the sponsorship has been chosen for other marketing (or personal) reasons, and free tickets just happen to be one of the perks, this is not the same as planned corporate entertainment.

Adding Value

Despite all the potential negatives involved with spectator events, they still remain an enduringly popular part of the corporate entertainment spectrum. A client who wants to use them effectively, however, must be prepared to look at ways of adding value.

One way is to dress the day in luxury, using limousines and private helicopters to avoid the crowds, private facilities that afford better views than would be generally available to the public, and lavish meals.

A better way is to involve the guests in the event in some way. Say, for instance, that you have invited them for a day at the races. By inviting them to arrive a few hours earlier than the rest of the crowds, you can take them round the course with one of the jockeys, who can explain what happens at each jump and why one is more dangerous than another. They could then be introduced to some of the trainers and the horses that are going to be running.

Once they have some of this background, guests will become more actively involved in the day, understanding fully what is going on and feeling part of it. Simply watching a number of horses run round a track is not particularly exciting unless you stand to win or lose a lot of money on the result, but if you are watching 'your jockey', or the horse you thought looked fit to win, or were tipped to watch by a trainer or owner, you will be agog. Your heart will be in your mouth when you see the horse stumble at a fence and you will be cheering when it triumphs.

In Simon Morris's experience:

> Many companies buy space at a major event which might last four days or more, but they think to use it only on one or two of the days. As a result they miss opportunities. Either they could be arranging different types of events at the venue on the other days, or they could be selling on the space they don't want to someone else, or even giving it to a charity.
>
> We organised an event at the Royal Tournament one year and we arranged for the host company to bring along the guests on the days when the event was being set up and the performers were training and rehearsing, as well as on the days when the general public was there. It made the event far more memorable for the guests because it gave them a peek behind the scenes.

The same applies to car-racing or any other sport. Only by involving people and making them feel part of the excitement of the day will you make it a truly memorable experience. If you know what it feels like to be sitting in a Formula One car, have experienced the excitement in the pits and have driven round the route, or one like it, you are going to be more involved when the race starts.

There can, therefore, be advantages to overlapping a spectator event with a participative one. Suppose, for instance, that you have a client who is an avid tennis player and fan. If you invite them to a major international tournament one afternoon, and suggest that before lunch they might like to take some private tennis lessons with a famous professional on a private court near to the venue, you will have the basis of a memorable and exciting day.

The same could work with golf or any other sport that spectators tend to play to a high standard themselves.

With cultural events this might be harder, although a visit behind the scenes at an opera house, or to a rehearsal, will help to broaden the guests' understanding of what happens on stage, increase the pleasure they derive from the day and give them an extra reason to accept the invitation.

For the corporate entertainment beginner, a well-known spectator event can be a good place to start, but as many other companies will have the same idea, the more time and effort you put into making your package special, the greater the benefits will be.

Cavendish is a consultancy company that specialises in putting these sorts of events together (as well as the one-off special events). Jim Bignall has found:

> We make a commitment at something like a grand prix for 200 seats. We then have to fill those seats by offering added-value packages to clients. We do that at around forty different events, so that we have a calender that runs throughout the year and we can recommend the best events for the customers' particular needs. Our aim is to provide a consistent standard at each event, so that our customers know that they can expect certain things wherever they go with us.
>
> It is our job to make sure that the guests are entertained all through the day. If we are taking them motor-racing, for instance, we might set up a scalectrix model racing circuit in the hospitality chalet, and a driving simulator. This means that people won't just be standing around waiting for something to happen.

One of the biggest problems at participative events in the past has been black-market tickets, and although the corporate hospitality industry is trying hard to eradicate them, this is hard to do. In Britain the Wimbledon tennis authorities were the first to declare that their tickets were non-transferable. This meant that each day only the 2,000 or so debenture tickets that were openly traded on the stock market could be sold on to other people. Anyone else wanting corporate hospitality facilities had to buy packages from the official agency, Keith Prowse. This practice is likely to spread to other major events as the levels of professionalism improve throughout the industry.

Jim Bignall again:

> We want to provide a totally professional service to clients, and you can't do that with black-market tickets. Although we have all had to rely on them in the past, it has always been a risk. You can't be sure, for instance, that your seats will be together. That may mean you have to split your group up and send them all over the place, which will completely undo all the good work you may have done at building a group atmosphere. You may not even get seats, or at the worst, may not get into the venue at all if there is something wrong with the tickets.

If you buy a package from a company like Cavendish, everything you can expect to get will be laid out in black and white. The prices quoted should be inclusive and the running of the day will be taken completely out of your hands.

Itineraries will be personalised to your company, there will be reserved car-parking and company signage. You will get admission to the grounds and quality seating, and a complimentary bar will run throughout the day. The catering will be included, with special menus for people who prefer something different. They will also decorate the premises with flowers and themed table decorations, and organise celebrity speakers, sweepstakes, umbrellas and wet-weather contingency plans, closed-circuit and colour television facilities, programmes, mementoes of the day, tote vouchers and complimentary bets (for horse-racing events) and anything else the client wants.

Chapter summary

- Choose events with the right atmosphere.
- Take away all the anxieties and administrative problems of getting there for your guests.
- A famous event will not be enough on its own; it will need added value and marketing.
- Don't pick an event because you enjoy it; pick it to suit your guests.
- Events that you sponsor may not be the best for your corporate entertainment needs.
- Use your allotted space to maximum advantage.
- Involve guests and make them part of the event.

Chapter 10

Participative Events

'An activity day should be eagerly anticipated, well attended, much enjoyed, and long remembered,'
Sam Gill, managing director of Business Pursuits

While spectator sports, in conjunction with the business lunch, could be considered the foundation stones of the corporate entertainment industry, participative events are now seen by many as the way forward.

The image problem of the participative sector is largely based on fear of the unknown and of embarrassment. People are always afraid of making fools of themselves, and it is easier to sit in a seat and watch professionals doing something than actually have a go yourself.

Most people are frightened of failing and will consequently avoid anything that might lead them unnecessarily down that path. Many are also lazy and prefer to watch rather than participate.

At the same time, there are people who constantly need to be challenged and stimulated by new problems and experiences. In many cases these are the ones who are most successful in life, and consequently find themselves on the target lists of host companies.

An invitation to a participative event, therefore, needs to be couched in exactly the right terms for all types of target. It may be that some ideas are suitable for one sort and not another, but with the right amount of attention to detail it should be possible to make one event attractive to a wide range of different people.

Once again this brings us back to the crucial need for the host company to know and understand their targets, and to ensure that every event is tailored to suit their tastes exactly. An invitation to climb a mountain might excite one person, an invitation to see the view from the top might be the key to hooking someone else, while a third person might prefer to jump from the summit on a hang-glider. All three people could be accommodated on one day; equally, all three could refuse the invitation if the idea was put to them in the wrong way.

A participative event can range from a day on a golf course with two or three guests, or a day's falconry or archery, to 100 people going go-karting or ten-pin bowling. It could be an evening where your guests get to sample what it is like to be treated as a film star, or a rock star. It could be a wine-tasting at a famous vineyard, a day at a luxury health farm, or an opportunity to go out into the woods with paint-ball guns and shoot people. It could be a day's fishing on a luxury boat, or a day out shooting phea-sants. It could be a treasure hunt in a vintage car or a coaching session from a world-famous sports personality. It could be a chance to drive your dream car or to learn to fly a plane.

What the host needs to be offering is the chance to learn and experience something new, but it must be something that the target wants to learn or experience. At the same time, you need to demonstrate that what you are offering will be fun, and that the target will be spending the day with like-minded people.

As Eddie Hoare says:

> Inside every adult there is a child just dying to get out. I have had senior company executives standing in fields playing with remote-control toy cars and having the most wonderful time. It all comes down to the way you package the ideas.
>
> The same people might just as easily be tempted to a

wine-tasting in a cellar somewhere. They will be persuaded to come by the promise of a chance to drink some famous vintage. The fact that they will get only a mouthful or two is irrelevant – it has given them something to talk about, and it is something that they couldn't arrange for themselves.

Once they are there, they can then be given a highly entertaining time by a good master of wine, while simultaneously being educated. There are endless permutations with wine. You might, for instance, organise a tasting of the Chardonnay grape around the world, so that you have wines from every different country, and a master of wine to explain the differences. An event like that can be a simple cocktail-party-style affair, or it can be followed by a full-blown dinner, or it could be part of a full day's entertainment at a wonderful venue somewhere. The important thing is that the guests are impressed by the experience, entertained and educated.

If it is sufficiently well tailored, a participative event can be a way of catching the attention of people who would normally be virtually impossible to reach. The Profile Partnership, for instance, was charged by a client with the task of getting a group of influential city analysts to sit down in a room and listen to a presentation. After considerable research they came up with a package that involved inviting the targets to an exclusive resort in Switzerland for three days. The presentations took place on the first two days and on the third day the analysts were taken out on to the slopes with the ski instructor who had choreographed the skiing for a James Bond movie and a famous ski photographer. They could then be shown how to perform feats they had never done before, and be pictured in the process. All of them accepted the invitation.

According to Jim Bignall:

The outward-bound style of leadership courses can also be used for corporate entertainment purposes. I think it can be particularly useful if you have project teams put together from a variety of different companies who need to get to know one another and learn to work in unison. With major computer projects, for instance, there might be people from a client company, a software supplier, a hardware supplier and another consultancy. They may all be working together for some time, and they need some sort of opportunity to get acquainted at the beginning and to learn about one another's strengths.

These sorts of events can also be very useful for sales conferences, where the danger is that delegates will become bored when they are not actually in sessions. Just giving them a gala dinner and some celebrity cabaret star is not usually enough, but a day out doing something different can make a real impact and have some positive side effects on morale and team spirit.

Getting the Guest Mix Right

As with any other sort of entertaining, it may be that the other guests will act as part of the lure to your target. If, for instance, you are targeting chief executives of companies in a particular sector, the fact that one is going might encourage others who would welcome a chance to spend time with them. Just as people go to exhibitions and conferences to talk to other people in their industry, so they can be tempted to spend a day out with them. With a participative event, they know there will be more of a chance to get to know these people well.

If the event is being designed for internal corporate entertainment, it is vital that the marketing of the event to the guests does not make it seem like something compulsory. It is possible that ideally everyone should attend, and the event may be built into a training scheme that is compulsory, but it must still be stressed that this is something fun, something being provided as light relief, and something that has been designed to suit each target's individual tastes. People will then feel that they have volunteered, which means less chance of resentment.

Individual Tailoring

Spectrum Communications is one of the world's leading conference organisation companies. A major new client may be trusting them with a budget of hundreds of thousands, making them responsible for the launch of a new product or a communications plan that is integral to their success. If they are going to win new business, they have to be liked and trusted by the people using their services.

They are in a relatively competitive market, with competitors who can offer more or less identical services to theirs. The only way, therefore, that they can differentiate themselves is through their staff and the impression they make on potential and existing clients.

Consequently they operate a very low-key and successful corporate entertainment strategy, both to win new clients and to build relationships with existing ones.

The people who buy their services tend to be senior managers with huge companies, possibly even chief executives. The company targets these people very carefully. They will all be sophisticated individuals with full diaries who receive a great many invitations to corporate entertainment events and turn down the vast majority.

Managing director Paul Swan says:

> We find out, in the course of casual conversations, what their real passions are, and then we match them up to someone in the company who has similar passions. So, for instance, we are members of the Wentworth Golf Club, one of the most exclusive courses in the world and one that every keen golfer wants to play on. We also take a boat down to Cowes for the annual Cowes Regatta.

All they do is invite their targets, as individuals, to come out for a day's golf, or to join them as part of the team on the boat (or some other activity). If the target is a golf or sailing enthusiast, the invitation is not going to be easy to refuse. If the target has an interest not shared by one of their directors, Spectrum will find someone else in the company who is an enthusiast and put them together with the client. The people who are integral to the business relationship will still be involved, but the level of the event is kept high by having an expert there as well.

Paul Swan again:

> Golf is obviously a good way of getting to know people, because it is so relaxing and there is a lot of time for casual conversation, both on the course and at the club house over lunch. We also have a number of people in the company who enjoy it. With the boat it is rather different; it is excitement that we are offering. There is no five-star entertainment involved, they are going to be eating sandwiches on board with the rest of the crew, but as well as experiencing a world-class event from the inside, they also have an opportunity to see just how competent members of our team are, and to see them working under pressure.

The point is that the invitations must fit exactly the drives and tastes of each guest. For many people a day on a golf course would be a bore, while others would find the discomfort and danger of a boat race too intimidating. When it is easy enough for people to tell themselves they are refusing invitations they are quite attracted to because they are virtuous and are resisting temptation, no one will accept invitations to participative events that they don't even find attractive.

The Professional Activity Day

'The brief from clients usually starts with, "We want to do something different",' says Sam Gill, managing director of Business Pursuits, a company specialising in activity days that owns the majority of the equipment it uses. He lists the advantages of participative activities as he sees them:

- the ability to be different;

- greater flexibility – wherever and whenever;
- exclusivity;
- drink-free, healthy environments;
- a sense of achievement for the participants;
- an element of competition.

He explains:

Exclusivity means a number of things. I recently went to a major spectator event and it took me an hour and a half to get out of the car park at the end. So it means you avoid crowds and traffic problems. But it also means that you are not just one marquee like dozens of others; you are genuinely offering guests something individual and private.

In most cases Business Pursuits will hire a large country house with an estate, and will provide high-quality catering throughout the day.

Sam Gill again:

The perception of activity days can be a problem, since people tend to think of them as muddy, messy and downmarket. That is a complete myth and you can dispel it by getting the right location and image. The food can be far better than at a large event, and the catering staff will be much fresher since they haven't been worked off their feet for days on end.

It is important that the hosts find out what sort of sports the guests are interested in. If they work in the financial sector, that sort of thing will probably have come up in the course of the many telephone conversations they have every working day. If they don't know the tastes of their targets, then it is worth writing round and asking. It is a good idea if the hosting client talks directly to the organisers like us, rather than leaving it to their agent. That way we can ask them all the relevant questions, and can ensure that the brief is as full as possible. We need to know why they are holding the event, who for, how many of them, and demographics like their likely age range, job titles, gender and so on. We also need to know what time of year they would prefer.

There is never any problem with the entertainment side of it;

the tricky bit is getting people to attend. If someone receives thirty or forty invitations a year and accepts only three or four, you have to make sure yours is one of the most tempting.

Sam Gill believes that one of the mistakes host companies make is not advising people of the quality of the day. Guests are asked to an activity day full stop. If instead they were to be sent pictures of the sort of equipment they would be using, a brochure about the venue and perhaps an itinerary telling them what would be happening, they would get a better picture of what was in store and why they should attend.

> Photographs can be very powerful, pointing out to them that they could be sitting in that actual seat themselves. You can even send them videos of the vehicles in action to give them a taste of the atmosphere and excitement.
>
> Once the guests have accepted the invitations, we can supply clients with standard texts to send out before the event to keep their interest and make sure they know where to come and what to bring, and not to be put off if it is raining because the event will be designed to cater for such eventualities.

Companies like Business Pursuits actually have to prove their worth by inviting potential customers to come on their days in order to test them. Sam Gill has discovered that if you are inviting potential clients you can expect a 25 per cent no-show. Which means that if he is looking to raise thirty people, he will invite forty.

> How many acceptances you get will depend on the quality of the invitation, and also on the quality of the relationship between the host and the guest. People tend to accept invitations from people they like more readily.
>
> When people arrive on one of our standard days, we will divide them into teams (probably four teams of six people each), and they will have forty minutes practising each of the activities – say archery, riding Honda pilot racers and quad bikes, and clay-pigeon shooting – in the morning. They will have a three-course lunch (with no drink because of the

dangers of the equipment), and then come out and compete in their teams at each of the activities. The day finishes with tea and prize-giving and a glass of champagne.

Putting people into teams increases the fun element and gives a purpose to the afternoon. It means that when they aren't actually doing an activity themselves, they can be cheering their team-mates on. To begin with we used to have overall champions for the day, but we stopped that as it took away from the team spirit, making everyone compete against everyone else. Now we usually have a prize for each activity and for an overall winning team. The prize-giving is always light-hearted, with booby prizes, and everyone goes away with something.

We believe it is better for clients to use companies that own their own equipment because that should make it cheaper (cutting out the middlemen), and we also have experience in the best way to make the days flow – getting the team sizes right, for instance, so that people are kept busy and not left hanging around. You want to aspire to a mixture of professionalism, informality and organisation, which is a difficult balance to get unless you have a lot of experience. Safety is highly important, but so is amusement and entertainment, so instructors need to be performers too.

The visual presentation of the day is important, from the uniforms the instructors wear to the state the vehicles are in and the way that the courses are laid out.

A package from a company like Business Pursuits would normally contain the following:

- maps and directions;
- exclusive venue hire;
- flowers in the house;
- event tents and bunting;
- course layout and construction;
- helmets and overalls as required;
- safety stands and ear-defenders;
- all activities and instruction;

- full catering package;
- soft drinks throughout the day;
- team and individual competitions;
- personalised scorecards;
- a glass of champagne with prize-giving;
- engraved trophies and champagne prizes;
- event management.

Novelty Value

The majority of participative events involve larger groups of people than a round of golf, and they are very much influenced by the fashions of the moment. At one time clay-pigeon shooting was still a novelty, as were war games and archery, and any opportunity to try them was bound to elicit a good response. Now they are standard forms of corporate entertainment and, although this doesn't mean they aren't effective, they no longer have novelty value. It probably takes around five years for a new idea to work its way down the market until virtually every likely corporate entertainment target has had a chance to try it. Even so, the people who love it will be happy to come back for more.

Sam Gill again:

> Clients sometimes worry about repeating themselves with the same activity. I don't believe that if someone has a wonderful time for a couple of hours a year, they won't want to repeat the experience the following year. People, after all, are happy to play golf for days on end, or to go back to the same holiday venues.

The driving of exotic vehicles over rough terrain is another area that is highly susceptible to fashion. When a new sort of vehicle comes on to the market, be it a quad bike, trial buggy, marine jet or single-seater hovercraft, it provides corporate hosts with new bait. Certain standard vehicles, however, like the Range Rover, are always popular and the manufacturers are usually very happy to provide support to a corporate entertainment event they think will be giving potential customers for their products a chance to test them under interesting conditions.

The point is that none of these events should be bought as a package just because they are new or convenient. Their novelty value may add to the reasons to purchase, but the event must fit in with an overall plan, both for the goals of the day and for the longer-term goals of the corporate entertainment plan.

Sometimes a tried and trusted – and a cheap – option can be highly effective. An evening spent go-karting in an old bus depot or on an ice rink somewhere, with simple barbecued food, might be considerably more effective for some audiences than a full day out at a grand venue.

Tailoring to Fit

Rather than buying an activity day off the shelf, it may be more suitable to contact one of the companies that organises such events, tell them what you are aiming to achieve and ask them to think up something special for you.

Kit Peters, managing director of Kit Peters Extraordinary Events, which specialises in just this type of operation, has found:

> People are constantly looking for new things to do. There are drawbacks to a lot of different activities, but there are ways of overcoming them. With sports like go-karting or hot-air ballooning, for instance, only a certain number of people can be doing the activity at any one time; the rest are left standing on the side-lines watching. You can get over this boredom factor by putting them into teams, so that the spectators are rooting for their side, but it is better if you can find something they can all do.

Peters has in the past organised activities like cannon- and musket-firing, with participants being taught how to use muzzle-loading muskets. To add a bit of colour, the day can then be themed around the activity, complete with roasting pigs, liveried servants and serving wenches. There are also 'woodland days', which involve problem-solving games and tricks like scaling trees with lumberjacks' equipment.

'Some companies do assault courses,' says Peters, 'but they can be very taxing physically for anyone who is not used to them, and they are only as exciting as you make them.'

Most people enjoy learning new skills, as long as they are confident they won't be made to look fools and that the people teaching them will be helpful and genuine experts in their field, be they Olympic marksmen or Formula One drivers.

Peters started in the corporate entertainment business by founding Skirmish, one of the most successful organisers of paint-ball games. The main lesson he learned from arranging Skirmish events for corporate clients was the high value to them of anything that built team spirit and broke down barriers between people. He was also struck by just how desperate many companies were for advice on how to work out exactly what they were trying to achieve. It is very easy to become so wrapped up in the administrative minutiae of organising an event that one forgets the initial purpose.

'Clients are sometimes more worried about making sure nothing goes wrong on the day than in creating something bold, wonderful and different,' he says. 'Guests will forgive the odd administrative hiccup if they are sufficiently excited by the overall concept.'

A software company approached Peters for ideas on how to make their three-day staff conference at a city-centre hotel into something memorable. Peters and his team responded by dreaming up a scenario which started with the 250 delegates all being told on the first evening to watch

127

television at seven o'clock the next morning in their hotel bedrooms. During the standard news broadcast from the station a fake item was inserted, telling them of the murder of a professor who was at the hotel to address their conference that day. The news item, which was presented by the station's normal newscaster, showed a drawing of the grinning corpse.

By the time they went downstairs for breakfast, the assembled company knew that they were in for something different. The whole day had been prepared like a giant, participative theatrical event. It was a murder story, complete with suspects played by actors and elaborate special effects and sets built in various conference rooms around the hotel.

The guests were divided up into sixteen teams, which then had to participate in eight different events, each run by one of the different characters. These characters ranged from a casino manager to Clint Eastwood, who 'happened to be visiting his sister in the hotel'. The successful teams were given clues to help them discover the identity of the murderer.

Each event was more elaborate and more complex than the one before. Some were intellectual puzzles to be solved, some were physically demanding, and others were both. All of them concentrated on breaking down barriers between the participants and gently moulding them into teams.

Kit Peters again:

> With all these things you get an element of cynicism at the beginning. After all, we are nearly always dealing with sophisticated and intelligent groups of people. As the events go on, however, it is wonderful to watch these people unwinding and getting into the spirit of the thing, completely forgetting their initial reservations. By the end of the event they were all leaping around and cheering, and in fact only two of the teams actually managed to crack the mystery, and only one of them got it exactly right.
>
> The costs can run high on these things, but it is usually more

important to get them right than to save money. We have a complete team of carpenters and electronic, mechanical, sound and video engineers, and highly equipped workshops. We are creating theatrical events, from the initial concept through the scripting to the final production. This event, for instance, involved a rooftop set, constructed in one of the hotel conference rooms, which the delegates had to get across with a series of pulleys and wires, negotiating a simulated 100-foot drop on the way. In the other rooms we had major assault courses, bucking broncos and a game involving a giant inflatable fruit salad!

Encouraging competition

While there are benefits to putting people into teams and having them compete, it is important that all competition remains light-hearted. If, for instance, there is going to be some sort of prize-giving at the end, then everyone must be involved, with joke prizes as well as real ones. It is vital that no one comes away from the day with a sense of failure. Rather, they must feel that they have learned something interesting, achieved something personally and enjoyed themselves. Then, provided that you have managed to get across your message, you will have succeeded.

Television Packages

A good way of tempting people to play games is to use a package that has appeared on television. From *Mastermind* to *The Krypton Factor*, from *Treasure Hunt* to *Sale of the Century*, you can adjust the games to suit your audience, while still retaining the basic atmosphere of the famous original. It makes the concept easier to package and sell if it is already known, and gives you the opportunity to link in with famous presenters.

Chapter Summary

- Overcome all fears of embarrassment and failure.
- Package and market the event to appeal to the individual targets.
- Offer the opportunity to learn and experience something new.
- Entertain your guests while educating them.
- Incorporate entertainment with training courses, conferences and other team-building exercises.
- Get the guest mix right.
- don't let staff believe events are compulsory; convince them that they want to come.
- Get the numbers right so that everyone can be kept busy all the time.
- It doesn't have to be for groups; it can also be for individuals.
- Use professional organisations with their own equipment for large-scale activity days.
- Keep competition friendly.
- Make sure invitees appreciate the quality of the event, using photographs and brochures.
- Check and double-check all safety procedures.
- Make sure the visual presentation of the day is of high quality.
- Novelty value is not enough on its own.

Chapter 11

Travelling Abroad

'Overseas activities increasingly represent an exciting opportunity to influence clients. Contrary to popular belief, these need not be too expensive.'

The Effectiveness of Corporate Hospitality,
BMSL Reports

The chance to travel to a foreign destination may well act as a useful hook for attracting targets. However, it will never work on its own. No one who is worth inviting to a corporate entertainment event will come just because it is being held in Hawaii, Rio de Janeiro or Monte Carlo, but if all the other ingredients in the mix are right, then a pleasant or interesting destination may make one invitation stand out from the rest.

David Tonnison, whose company the Marketing Organisation has a subsidiary called the Travel Organisation, has found:

The use of an exotic foreign location must be the culmination of a marketing campaign, not the opening shot. If you are running a customer motivation scheme, for instance, with the intention of making your company better known to a group of key potential clients, you might decide to use Barbados as the final destination. This is the pinnacle you are working towards and you will have to be highly subtle in the build-up. If you make it too big or obvious too soon, they will not come.

As the campaign progresses, you may be able to see that there are twenty individuals who really matter to you, people who have the ability to put enough business your way to fulfil all your dreams, and who are also likely to use you. Your aim now is to get time with these people, face to face, to ensure that they know what your company does, and that they remember you in the right way. It might take only ten minutes of your time to get that message across, but it has to be done in the right atmosphere and with the right groundwork. Just inviting them out to lunch will not make you stand out from the opposition – and anyway, they probably wouldn't accept the invitation.

Let's imagine you have succeeded in getting these twenty people down to Barbados for four days, with their spouses. It is now crucial to ensure that you get ten minutes with each one to put across your case. That doesn't mean hard sell; it means achieving your goals. So senior directors from the host company must be there to do the talking, and they must be completely familiar with the profiles of all twenty people, and they must know exactly when and how they are going to get their results during the trip. It may have cost several thousand pounds to get each of those ten-minute segments, and the money will be well spent if they are successful. But nothing must go wrong.

Export Marketing

Companies that are highly sophisticated at marketing within their own country are often completely lost when it comes to breaking into foreign markets. Corporate entertainment can be a highly cost-effective way of proceeding, provided that you have managed to isolate your potential customers, and are willing to travel to their country and stage an event that will attract their attention.

The initial groundwork and research may have been done by a sales team or an agent, but the actual forging of the relationship between the company and the prospective client can be achieved by entertaining. The novelty value of a foreign country, coupled with the attractions of the event itself, and the evident determination on the part of the hosts, will all help to give the potential customers the right impression.

Internal Incentives

Foreign travel is most used in the motivation of in-house employees. In this situation the straightforward chance of a trip to a dream destination could well be the carrot that stimulates people into trying harder to achieve certain goals. It is with in-house incentives, therefore, that the bulk of international corporate entertainment happens, particularly to long-haul destinations.

Even in that situation, however, glamour alone is not enough. There must be other reasons for the trip if it is to be an effective part of a corporate entertainment package. It may be that it fits into the theme of a motivation scheme, or that the destination provides the employer with an opportunity to put specific messages across to the guests; or it may be that that destination is the only place with enough hotel rooms and catering facilities for a party of that size.

When entertaining customers or prospective customers it is always worth looking at the options of travelling to another country, as long as you don't expect the trip to be a sufficient lure in itself.

The Advantages and Disadvantages

As far as advantages go:

- Invitations to travel will demonstrate that the host is willing to spend time and money entertaining guests, which means that they are considered important.
- A foreign destination may add an edge of glamour to the event.
- Foreign locations may simply be the most practical,

especially if the event is designed to attract guests from a number of different countries, or if it is linked to an international conference or exhibition, when the guests will have other reasons for being in that place.

- If the targets can be lured away from their home countries, there will be greater opportunities for talking and building relationships. If they are unable to head home in the evenings, they are bound to be a more captive audience.

- The options for the sort of events you can organise widen as soon as you decide that you can travel abroad. You immediately have a wider choice in everything, including the climate.

- Events organised in foreign destinations can *sometimes* be cheaper than those in a home country, despite the added costs of air fares and hotel accommodation.

- You are more likely to be able to create an event that is unusual and tempting to the target.

As to the disadvantages:

- Travelling takes up time, which is often the one thing your targets can least afford to spend.

- The event is likely to be more complicated, and organising and administering it may therefore take up more of your time.

- An invitation to a foreign destination that is not linked to a specific reason for being there, such as a factory visit or a conference, is likely to look more like a direct bribe.

- Foreign destinations generally push the costs up because they take longer to reach and therefore involve accommodation. (The average incentive trip costs about four times as much as the average corporate hospitality day held in the home country.)

There are, then, more advantages than disadvantages, but the latter are so great that for most corporate entertainment events travel is limited to anywhere that can be reached, and returned from, within a day, or possibly a weekend. In some cases companies will put a journey time-limit on it. They may say, for instance, that all events must be within two and a half hours' travelling time of the home country. The main reason for this is jet lag, which means not only that you need to stay away longer to make people feel comfortable but also that people are less effective than usual for several days after their return.

In both America and Europe the tradition for many companies has been to remain within their own continent, since both can provide a wide range of destinations, and only in recent years have long-haul flights begun to be used, as people become more experienced and need more variety to attract them. The improvement in jet travel has also had an impact. The fact that you can now fly non-stop from Europe to the Far East and beyond brings many new destinations within reach of corporate entertainers.

Sarah Webster, manager of the Incentive Travel and Meetings Association, finds:

> The tourist industry is very keen to encourage this sort of travel, largely because it can be used to sell their destinations in the months either side of the peak holiday periods, when the holiday-makers are not coming in sufficient numbers to fill the hotels. There are some destinations, like Monaco, that are simply not interested in the individual tourist and want to deal only in large numbers.

Why Choose a Foreign Destination?

To begin with there might be a definite reason to justify a trip. It may be, for instance, that your business is located in various different countries. If your products are made in Thailand, or you run a chain of hotels in the Caribbean, then it is not hard to see the reasoning behind taking a group of people to those destinations to see how the products are made, or to sample the delights of your establishments. While your guests are in the country, it is only courtesy that you should show them the sights, take them shopping or do whatever else is necessary to entertain them outside working hours.

If your business is internationally based, you will also have reasons for using overseas venues. You might, for instance, arrange for guests to visit one of your client sites to see your products or services in action. Or you might organise an event in a destination that would be central for a number of your clients from different countries, or where you know they visit often.

If there is a high educational content in the event that you are planning, such as a conference or seminar, which is bound to take more than one day anyway, then there is no reason why you shouldn't locate the event at a foreign destination. The medical and legal professions, for instance, are used to travelling to exotic destinations for their conferences.

National Boundaries Don't Have to Be Barriers

National boundaries are sometimes misleading. We tend to think that in crossing a border we are travelling further. An American company might, for instance, be closer to Acapulco than Chicago; a British company might be closer to Paris than to Newcastle. Nor is it just a question of miles. If the destination you are aiming for is close to an airfield, travelling time will be far less than that spent on a busy road in your own country.

The impression that you can give to your targets, however, by inviting them to cross a national border for lunch, dinner or whatever can be dramatic. A wine-tasting held at a famous French château will be considerably more alluring than one held at a hotel in Amsterdam. A day's golf on a course overlooking the Gulf of Mexico will have more appeal than a day on a course in Detroit. A trip on the Orient Express will be better than an internal commuter flight.

National boundaries should not be seen as barriers; rather, it is the travelling time spent getting there and back that is the potential obstacle.

Chartering a Plane is Cheaper Than You Think

People who are not used to international travel tend to think of themselves as being trapped by scheduled airlines and major airports, when in fact chartering a private plane could be a far better and cheaper alternative.

On any scheduled air trip the hours actually spent flying from A to B often make up less than half the real journey time. If you think about it, you have to get to an international airport early, in order to be sure you have no problems on the way. You then have to check in, board, wait for permission to take off, wait for permission to land, wait to be ferried to the terminal, queue with all the other passengers from all the other planes for passport control and customs, and then find transport to take you to your final destination. You will probably add at least three hours to any trip, presuming that everything goes smoothly. You will certainly add a great deal of aggravation and anxiety.

Suppose instead that all you had to do was drive to an airfield near your home or office, park your car and walk out to a plane that was waiting just for you. The plane takes off as soon as you are on board, and when you land at an airfield close to your destination, there is a car waiting to take you on the last leg of the journey. In this way you will immediately have brought within reach a number of destinations for one-day events that would otherwise have been impossible. Light planes can fly from and to literally thousands of different airfields that no scheduled plane ever gets to, one of which is bound to be near to your chosen destination.

Provided that you have enough people to fill a small plane, the seats will not work out any more expensive than those for scheduled flights to the same destination, and in many cases they will be a great deal cheaper. If it is a one-day event, the plane will simply wait at the airfield to fly back when you are ready.

The other great advantage of chartering is flexibility with regard to timing. Guests can leave when they want and return when the event is over. If it runs late and they were booked on to a scheduled flight, either the hosts would have to spoil the effect of the event by cutting it short, or there would be the inconvenience of getting on to a later flight or the extra cost of accommodation.

There are dozens of different types and sizes of charter aircraft, all of which provide different degrees of benefit and prestige. (In fact, there is no reason why you shouldn't charter Concorde if your budget can stand it and you can justify the expense in marketing terms.)

If you have your own plane, you can customise it in any way you want, change the in-flight service, or use the flying time to talk to guests, hand out information and brief them on what is going to happen during the day.

Above all, however, it is the impression a private plane gives that is so significant. It demonstrates an acknowledgement on the part of the host company that their guests are important and their time valuable.

Helicopters, while considerably more expensive than planes, can also play a part in an event. They are particularly useful for taking people short distances that would normally be affected by traffic jams and queues. A popular race track, for instance, will always have a helipad available for companies wishing to bring important guests in and out quickly. This sort of touch at an event like a racing day can make all the difference between the ordinary and the special. One company used helicopters every year to take people racing, until they needed to economise in some way and decided to opt for coaches. The response to their invitations dropped by over 50 per cent as a direct result, and they went back to helicopters the next year.

The main drawback to helicopters is that they cannot fly in very bad weather, so you will need to lay on alternative ground transport as a back-up. If the helipad is more that a few yards from the hospitality area, you will probably be using coaches or cars of some sort anyway, so they can easily take over in a crisis.

The Image of the Destination

If you are using a foreign destination as a hook to get guests to accept an invitation, or to motivate staff, then the image of the destination must be right. Once again, though, it isn't everything, and the infrastructure also has to be able to provide the sort of services that the host needs to make things run according to plan.

In practice there are a limited number of destinations with the sort of glamour that will add to an event and can also give the right levels of service and reliability. To begin with the climate has to be right. In the spring and autumn, for instance, it is risky to use beach resorts in Europe, so this limits organisers to the cities. For beaches you then have to look to the Caribbean, Florida, California, Hawaii, Australia and the South Pacific or Kenya. The Far East is also a useful area, providing exciting cities with excellent hotels, and beautiful beaches at the right times of the year.

There are certain marvellous destinations that host companies have to avoid because they don't convey the right image. India, for example, would be great, but corporate hosts don't want their guests exposed to the poverty. In North Africa they are suspicious of the food, and South

America is also considered dangerous by many companies whose guests are unused to the area.

Political unrest is another reason for ruling out the use of a particular destination. Israel, for instance, can offer visitors virtually anything they want, but in the minds of most people who have never been there it is a dangerous, war-torn country. Unrest in any part of the world can put people off travelling. Visitors from America to Europe virtually vanished during the 1991 Gulf War, although there were in fact no terrorist incidents.

Corporate hosts simply can't afford to take risks, and there are enough trouble-free destinations for them to choose from.

The most important factor in any travel equation is first-class hotels with de-luxe facilities. This tends to rule out places like West Africa, unless you are going to take the whole event under your control and organise a tented safari with all the attendant excitements. Basically, people want to go to glamorous and exciting places but they don't want any of the discomforts or dangers of real travel. It helps if local people speak the language of the guests, and it is difficult if the places are thought of as being dull, even if that perception is wrong in reality.

As Sarah Webster says:

Canada suffers badly from its image of being dull, cold and with nothing but the great outdoors to offer. But if you can package it cleverly, including things like the Rockies and the Calgary Stampede, you can still make it attractive and make use of the excellent infrastructure.

It is just as important to ensure that a destination suits the tastes of the guests. Festivals, for instance, can be a great draw, but it is no good taking a group of serious-minded individuals to the festival in Rio because they are not going to want to spend five solid days partying. The same group probably won't want to drink for a week at a German beer festival either. For others these events might be perfect.

In most cases it has to be a trip that the guests couldn't or wouldn't organise for themselves, and these days, when most of the potential targets for corporate entertainment have been travelling abroad on work and holidays for many years, this has become increasingly difficult.

Sarah Webster again:

Keeping the image of a destination while catering for large numbers can be a problem, but it can be done with careful marketing and by building the right facilities. In a destination like Monte Carlo, for instance, there are hotels with entrance lobbies that are used by the rich and famous, and then separate entrances for groups to check in at. So Joan Collins or James Goldsmith can be signing out at one desk, while several hundred fried-chicken sales people are being signed in somewhere else.

You can do this sort of thing only in destinations that are at a mature stage of evolution in their infrastructure. It isn't just the hotels that have to be excellent; it is everything else as well. You need to have the right sort of transport available, for instance, with guides who speak the right languages and understand the people they are dealing with.

You also need to have a wide range of entertainment facilities. If a group is going to be in a destination for a few days they can't eat in the same hotel every night, however good the food is. They have got to have something exciting to do each day, which can be themed and made different. If you have a group of 600 people – which is not unusual – that can be difficult to arrange in some destinations.

An element of fancy dress, for instance, can make an evening event into something that is talked about for months or years afterwards. Toga parties in Rome became a cliché in the 1970s, but they illustrate the point. All the guests would be invited to a toga party and would either be given a few basic props with which to make their costumes or be left completely to their own devices. When they arrived at the venue, wrapped in their bath towels and bed sheets, they would find the room decked out like a sumptuous Roman orgy, complete with reclining couches, giant bowls of fruit, tiled baths and Nubian slaves. The whole event would be themed to a level they would never see in the normal course of their lives.

What you need to do is find destinations that have a 'dream element'. It might be because of their beauty or their history, like a desert party in the rose-red city of Petra, or it might be because the rich and famous are thought to go there. There needs to be a perceived élitism, so that the travellers feel they are experiencing the best. It has to be somewhere they couldn't get to on their own, something offering exclusivity or novelty.

The dream element may not be borne out in reality, but that can be overcome. Acapulco, for instance, has a dream element because of its history and the very sound of its name. In reality it is a fairly tacky destination, but it has some wonderful resort hotels that more than live up to the image of glamour. If people are taken to these resorts, and then moved carefully to other gorgeous places for entertainment, they will be more than happy with the choice of destination. If they went to Acapulco under their own steam, they might well be disappointed.

Free Time

If a trip is to last more than one or two days, then the guests must be given free time for shopping, lying on the beach or taking advantage of whatever the local attractions are. If they want hire cars, there must be someone who can arrange it for them. Guests should never have to dig into their own pockets to pay for these sorts of extras. Private sightseeing tours should be arranged for those who want them, offering more than the commercial tours. At all times guests must feel that they are being lifted out of the ordinary crowd and being treated like important people.

'Some people like to entertain themselves,' says Sarah Webster, 'while others want to be coddled from start to finish. It is a question of knowing your customers and finding out what they want. It may be that they simply want some free time in order to go to bed and sleep for the afternoon.'

Taking Partners

On most trips it is advisable to include partners. Targets are much more likely to accept a trip if it doesn't mean leaving their partner behind and although men on stag trips may pretend to be having a great time drinking and watching the women in Las Vegas or Amsterdam, in reality the majority of them do not enjoy that kind of thing. If you bring partners along, it opens up an enormous number of possibilities with romantic bands in the evening and social gatherings that would be ludicrous if filled with unattached people mostly of one gender.

As Sarah Webster says:

> Including partners in a motivational scheme can be very powerful, but you need to know your people and there are dangers. It may be, for instance, that the partner your guest is bringing is not the partner they are married to, and a cheery letter from you to the spouse talking about all the excitements to come – or worse still, talking about the trip afterwards – could be disastrous.

Some companies also include children in the packages, using destinations like Orlando. Once again, it helps to bait the hook, but it is important that separate programmes are arranged for the children, giving the parents time for adult entertainment.

Getting the Timing Right

The biggest hurdle to overcome is timing. People simply don't want to be away from their desks for longer than they have to be.

A four-day trip that can be arranged over a weekend, therefore, is more likely to attract people than one in the working week.

Get Professional Help

It would be very foolhardy for any client to try to organise a foreign corporate entertainment trip themselves. There are just too many potential pitfalls for anyone who is not thoroughly experienced in business travel and familiar with the destination itself.

Sarah Webster again:

> The potential for getting it wrong is enormous, like arriving at the hotel with your guests and finding there is no booking, or finding that you are met at the airport by pre-war buses rather than the air-conditioned coaches you were expecting, or not being met at the airport at all.
>
> Every client should 'walk the course' with the organisers. That means going to the hotels and seeing the facilities, trying out every leg of the journey. If you are going to be taking people on a coach trip, you need to do it yourself to see that it isn't too gruelling, and to check that it fits into your timetable. If you are going on safari, you must see the tents and vehicles, test the meals and meet the guides.
>
> A good on-the-ground operator can completely change the way things work. Imagine, for instance, that you have a group of 100 people in Thailand. You are due to fly home from Bangkok but the flight is delayed by nine hours. If you get it wrong you will be stuck with these people in a seething pit of an airport and you will have ruined the whole effect of the trip. A good ground operator, however, would have discovered that the flight was delayed several hours before, found a hotel near the airport and organised rooms for people to rest in, with food and drink. 'Change of plan, everyone,' they can say. 'Get your swimming costumes out – we've got another nine hours and we're off to the Shangri La.' They can then organise for the guests to be checked on to the flight from the air-conditioned comfort of the hotel, while they swim, drink, sleep, eat or do whatever they enjoy, confident that other people are looking after them.
>
> Good ground operators can turn potential problems into adventures. Bad traffic congestion in a city centre, for instance, could be avoided with jeeps taking people through the back

streets; an organised sightseeing tour round a red-light district before dinner will avoid people wandering around and being unpleasantly propositioned if they don't want to be.

When people are taken on organised trips, they expect to be looked after. That often means that they take a great deal less care than they would if they were travelling independently, drinking more, eating different foods and worrying less about being on time. That is one of the reasons you are taking them – to allow them to relax and enjoy themselves; it is also why you have to make sure that they are looked after and protected at every turn.

As David Tonnison says:

When I first go to see a client, I say, 'Don't tell me where you want to go, just tell me why and with whom. Then we can talk around a few destinations that might be appropriate in style, perception, quality and price.' If we come up with a destination that I don't know intimately, I will then send someone out to look at the options. When the initial report comes back, I will then travel out with the client, who is the only one who can ultimately decide if a venue is right or not. When we have made a decision, the client can go to the swimming pool and I can start to do some negotiating.

It is important to find places that the guests can see only the best people know about, and to do things the existence of which other people might not even be aware of. This means that you must have inside information about a destination; otherwise you will be relying on received ideas that may be years out of date or wholly inappropriate to your guests. Reading a travel article in a consumer magazine does not make you an expert on an area.

Once the decisions have been made, our main task is to keep checking things, looking for problems and potential problems, and looking for enhancements that will result in increased goodwill towards the host company. If one of the guests will be having a birthday during a trip, for instance, we need to know so that we can do something about it. If we know what business they are in, we might be able to arrange for a visit to something similar in the destination that will really excite and interest them, although it would be of no interest to anyone else. Little things like this will make an enormous difference.

Building a Trip into Something Bigger

A foreign destination, therefore, is just one more element in the planning of a corporate entertainment event, providing the planners with a wider range of opportunities for creative thinking. There are any number of examples of creative incentive travel schemes from all over the world, so let's just take one example to illustrate how an event can be built up.

A well-known British insurance company decided to take 1,200 people from Britain to Monaco. To begin with the group was divided up into three; some met in Paris and rallied down to the destination in hired cars, with a treasure hunt and gourmet meals at top hotels along the way; others, choosing a more leisurely option, took the train and spent three days in Avignon tasting wine, cruising on the river and walking; and the rest flew straight to Nice.

The rally was started and finished by racing driver Stirling Moss, and the company's top performer got to travel with him.

Once in Monte Carlo a number of different events were on offer, including a game show based on *It's a Knockout*, a gala dinner and cabaret hosted by TV personality Bob Monkhouse, and a beach party and flying display with helicopters and a jump jet.

During the day there was coaching provided by major tennis stars, and water-skiing from a luxury cruiser.

The gala dinner was hosted at the Monte-Carlo Sporting Club, which has a roof that slides back above diners to reveal the night sky. At the end of the meal there was a massive surprise firework display.

Not many companies can afford to arrange quite such a lavish trip, but organisers who have experienced these sorts of affairs can provide the inspiration for others to learn from, and give the industry the know-how it needs to be able to package events of all shapes and sizes anywhere in the world.

Chapter Summary

- Use corporate entertainment for export marketing.
- A trip can act as the pinnacle of a major campaign.
- The destination alone will not be enough; it must be relevant and marketed effectively.
- Foreign locations can be the most practical.
- National boundaries don't have to be barriers.
- You must overcome time factors.
- Chartering planes is cheaper than you think.
- Look for the dream element, then the infrastructure.
- Ensure guests have enough free time.
- Always include partners where possible.
- Always get professional help on foreign territory.
- Always 'walk the course' yourself, from start to finish.

Chapter 12

Celebrities and Experts

The presence of a celebrity at an event can help to bait the hook, but there must be a genuine and relevant reason for their being there. They must, in other words, contribute to the event, doing more than simply turning up and shaking a few hands. The only situations in which a celebrity can be 'tacked on' to the end of an event is if they have been hired simply as cabaret or MC for the occasion, in which case they can be bought and evaluated just like any other part of the event, from the wine to the car-parking facilities.

A professional MC can help enormously with any sort of event involving large groups that at some stage are going to be sitting as an audience listening to speeches or question-and-answer sessions. Handling that sort of situation is a very skilled job and the people who do it on television or radio are usually the most highly experienced in the field. The fact that they are also well known to the audience is really just a bonus, helping to show how very seriously the host company is taking the event. Their services are expensive if seen as fees for individual people, but when treated as another item, like catering or venue-hire, they are not outrageous.

People Who Can Teach

People enjoy meeting experts who can teach them something new, whether it is a jockey, a motor racer, a mountain

148

climber, an Olympic marksman or a chef. If that expert is also an entertaining personality, capable of leading a group and generating laughter, then the hosts have a bonus.

The Profile Partnership, for instance, uses an ex-Camel Trophy driver to train people in off-road driving skills. Although his forte is not really presentation, he is highly skilled at dealing with people on a one-to-one basis. As Simon Morris explains:

> He can persuade a know-all executive to try things his way, or persuade someone who is flatly refusing to drive over a cliff to trust him. He is able to get people trying things they would never dream themselves capable of, and afterwards they feel wonderful.
>
> Someone like that can make the difference between a successful day and a failure.

If on top of that the expert is also a well-known face from the media, that is yet another bonus. It means guests can go away and talk about their experiences, and those listening will immediately know the names. This gives guests greater scope for boasting and improves the impact of the day for the host.

What you want, therefore, is an expert. If that expert is also famous it will be easier to sell him or her to your targets.

If, however, a host has a choice between someone famous and someone who is able to mix well with people and is willing to put time and effort into making the event go well, the latter must always win out. There are people who, simply because they have appeared on television, trade on their celebrity. They hire themselves out simply to act as a 'draw' to events. It may work for opening supermarkets and other functions that involve getting as many of the general public there as possible, but it does not work for serious corporate entertainment. The celebrities merely look ridiculous and guests are disappointed to find that the famous are just like them.

Everyone Has Their Price

Virtually anyone can be cajoled into attending a corporate entertainment event. From the White House to Buckingham Palace, the stars will turn out if they are approached in the right way, but that doesn't mean that they will give value for money.

A company that wants to hire a member of the British Royal Family, for instance, can do so by making the approach early enough to the right people and by offering to make the right size of donation to the right charity. The easier it is for that person to attend the event, the better the chances of their accepting. So a visit to a polo match in which Prince Charles is planning to play anyway could well be enhanced by persuading the Prince to shake hands and chat to guests. You will not, however, get much of his time and it will be impossible to insist that he put across any sort of coherent corporate message. If you wanted to invite the Queen of England to an event, you would have to make an equally large donation to her chosen charity, and you would also need to be a cause or company of which she approved.

According to Chas Wheeler:

> A European computer company was bringing a number of its best clients to London for a conference and they wanted to take them to a polo match on the last day. They wanted to meet Prince Charles. We fitted their event into a charity match and he came into the marquee afterwards and chatted to the guests for forty minutes. That sort of thing will always be a pull because so few people have actually met the Royal Family.

And Eddie Hoare adds:

> Clients are always asking if we can get a member of the Royal Family for them, but they seldom have any idea just how expensive it will be, or how difficult to arrange. There is also the problem that senior royalty work to their own rules, and you can't expect them to work to yours, however much money you are donating.

An approach to a major politician could also be helped with a donation to that person's political party.

Professional organisers get to know the VIPs who work the hardest, and so tend to use them regularly. They are also aware of the snob appeal, particularly in Europe, that a title can add to a gathering. Inviting guests to a castle in Germany or Scotland for a fine meal and a day of country sports is always a popular type of event. Its cachet will be increased, however, if the invitation is from the owner of the castle – particularly if they happen to be a lord or a count, and if they can be relied upon to mix with guests and help them to enjoy their day.

There are no golden rules as to who will and who won't be willing to work in this way. Some senior aristocrats are quite happy to give their time free to guests if they happen to be there on the day, but are not willing to commit themselves to a definite arrangement. Others openly include their personal services as part of the package on offer. And others again are willing to make a personal contribution only by special arrangement.

Eddie Hoare again:

> A title is always helpful in adding cachet to an invitation. There is no doubt that an invitation from a lord is likely to get a higher response than one from an unknown aristocrat. People like to take advantage of an invitation to puff up their own social status. They like to be able to talk about 'having lunch with Lord Ponsonby at his place last week', without mentioning that it was organised by a supplier of theirs and there were 100 other people in the same dining room. People like to feel that they are having a glimpse into a world that would normally be out of their reach. We ran a series of events called 'Behind Closed Doors', which was very successful because it got people into places they would never have been able to get into in any other way.

Building an Event around a Celebrity

In some cases it may be that a celebrity expert so epitomises a certain subject that an event can be built around them. A famous chef, for instance, can spend a day with a group of guests, taking them to the markets in the early morning to show them how to choose and buy the best ingredients, and then allowing them into the kitchens to demonstrate how a five-star meal is prepared. The guests would then be able to go through to the dining room for their meal with an increased understanding of what they are ordering and eating.

In Chapter 10 I explained how an expert can help to involve people in the events of the day, and the same is true with wine-tasting or rally-driving, sky-diving or gardening. It doesn't matter what the subject is, as long as the guests have a burning interest in it and the expert can increase their knowledge, understanding or enjoyment of it.

It is important that any VIP who is invited is not too powerful a figure for the personalities of the host company to compete with. A really powerful celebrity can eclipse the host company in the memory of the guests. If all they are going to remember is that they met George Bush or John Major, then the host has failed to achieve the prime objective of the project, which should be to build a relationship with the guests. If the VIP's presence is too powerful, it might push the whole event off balance.

There can also be hidden disappointments. One organiser tells the story of how he persuaded Princess Diana to open a building for a client in London, and was delighted by the huge crowd of press photographers who turned up to record the event. Unfortunately, that evening she went on to another event at which she wore a daringly low-cut silver evening dress, and it was pictures of this that appeared in all the papers the following day.

Careful advance liaison with the equerries who oversee the diaries of the Royal Family can help you to anticipate these sorts of catastrophes, although there is little you can do to avoid them.

Sharing Them out

The danger with any VIP is that a few of the strongest characters in the group will monopolise them, creating an élite 'inner group' that will make other people feel left out. This has to be guarded against at all costs and can be avoided with good planning and management.

If the expert is there to teach them something specific, then it is important that he or she spends an equal amount of time with everyone, and a group should not be so big that this is impossible.

If there is a VIP at an event where there will be a sit-down meal, it is hard to avoid the creation of an élite top table. The important thing in that situation is to make it clear to everyone from the beginning whether they will or will not be sitting on that table.

As Paul Swan says:

> It is always a good idea to have a few 'standy-by' VIPs, just in case someone who is designated to sit at the VIP table doesn't turn up. What you don't want to do is take someone off one table and 'move them up', because that will cause resentment among all the others who are left behind. You should not, however, leave any gaps on the top table, as that will suggest that the event is not going as planned.
>
> From the beginning the organisers need to take aside one or two people who they know very well, and who they can trust not to let their egos get in the way, and ask them if they would mind being stand-by VIPs. That means that they basically hover around in the background in case there is a gap at the top table, in which case they will be discreetly brought in to fill it. If no gaps appear, the stand-bys can sit at another designated table for 'friends of the management', such as the organising staff.

Always Get References

If you are hiring a professional celebrity (as opposed to a Royal or a politician), it is always worth talking to other people who have used their services in the past, to find out if they are the best person for the job. If the event is going to be at a sporting venue, then the venue management may also be able to suggest people who are good value. Never be so dazzled by someone's celebrity that you forget they are simply selling a professional service like anyone else, the product being themselves.

If a celebrity is not particularly good with people – and some aren't – you may still be able to find a way of using them in conjunction with a professional presenter. Chas Wheeler tells of a well-known jockey who was not particularly good at standing up and talking, so they hired a television presenter and sat the two of them down for a question-and-answer session. This gave the audience two celebrities instead of one, and added an air of polish and professionalism to the proceedings that would otherwise have been missing.

Chapter Summary

- Professional presenters help the flow of a formal event.
- Expertise is more valuable than celebrity status.
- Experts need to be entertainers as well.
- Famous faces can give guests another ticket to boast.
- Beware! A big name may outshine the hosts.
- People like to see 'behind closed doors'.
- Always share the celebrities out fairly among the guests, and plan their every move.
- Always check their references.

Chapter 13

Getting the Results

According to Simon Morris 'A host should be able to get a guest to sign an order while still at the event – provided that is the brief for the project.'

In most cases there is not such a specific tactical brief involved in a corporate entertainment event (and in some cases it would be sacrilege to talk business at all), but the theory still stands even if the goals are strategic, because sooner or later an organiser is going to have to justify the costs of the project to someone. To do that they must be clear about what the goals were and be able to measure their success against them.

As Eddie Hoare says:

> The problem is that you can seldom equate sales with a corporate entertainment project. It may be that you meet someone new at an event, get to know them well enough to be able to ring them up a week later on first-name terms, and that the relationship ends up producing business. The accountants in your company won't know about that connection unless you explain it to them. They will simply want to know how much product you managed to sell immediately as a result of the investment.

'Sometimes it can take up to two years before a potential client who has been invited to a corporate entertainment event actually makes a purchase,' says Chas Wheeler, 'but at other times the orders will come through the next week.'

There are so many things to think about when organising a corporate entertainment event, and so many things that could go wrong, that organisers who have managed to get through the day without any major catastrophes, and who have sent guests home smiling and grateful, could be forgiven sighing with relief and congratulating themselves on their success.

That, however, is simply an administrative success. The caterer can be congratulated for having created a good meal, and the waiters can be congratulated for keeping the drinks flowing, but the organisers will have completed their jobs only when they can be sure that the original goals have been met. This means the business objectives that the corporate entertainment is designed to achieve.

Corporate entertainers can be compared with the creators of a beautiful advertisement who may be proud of the great flair they have shown but will have fulfilled their brief only if that advertisement has the desired effect on the client's business, be it increased awareness or increased sales.

'Very few companies measure results,' says Philippa Bovey, 'which they could do if they had set up their criteria well in advance. Just having some way of monitoring the number of thank-you letters would be a start. Guests who have had a really good time will nearly always write and say so.'

It doesn't matter what the goals were, as long as they existed and were valid. For them to be effective, they need to be written down in the form of a brief that everyone involved can follow.

Having the Goals Written down

The aims of the campaign, as worked out at the beginning, must be written down somewhere. This brief should be referred to regularly along the way, to ensure that the problems of organising the event have not made you lose sight of the original goals. They should certainly be read carefully by everyone on the day before the event itself, as preparation for the real thing.

Your list of goals might, for instance, contain some of the following objectives:

- To get our top ten customers together for a day.
- To spend at least ten minutes talking individually to each of them.
- To let them know about changes in the company structure and how they will improve our service.
- To find out what they think of the company.
- To find out about any special needs they have which we could meet.
- To get to know each of them better.
- To let them know about a forthcoming price rise.
- To convince them they should renew their contracts.
- To sell them other products or services which they currently don't buy from the company.
- To persuade them to take out service contracts.
- To sell them a more expensive product.
- To dispel any misconceptions about the product.
- To overcome any particular barriers to purchase.

The organiser can then look back at this list at the end and see what has been achieved, and can also check the progress of the campaign as they go along. Have they, for instance, left enough time in the schedule to get the desired ten minutes with each of the targets? Have they made sure there will be enough people there from the host company who understand about the changes and can explain them convincingly? Does each person from the host company have some mechanism for recording the needs revealed by the targets? It is no good saying to a target in the middle of a conversation that you will speak to the distribution manager about getting their orders out more promptly if you then forget all about it. In the excitement of the event itself it is virtually impossible to remember every conversation, unless you make discreet notes to which you can refer afterwards when you are back at your desk.

Some of these questions will be easy to answer, like who your targets were and whether you managed to persuade them to turn up on the day. Others will be more subjective, like looking into how their perceptions of you may have changed.

'Not for one moment should anyone on the host team be thinking, "I'm here for a nice day out",' says David Tonnison. 'They are there to work and they must never forget that.'

Questions to be Asked

- Who were your original targets?
- How many of them accepted the invitation?
- How many of them turned up?
- How many of your target companies sent someone else?
- What were the impressions you wished to give this target group?
- Do you believe you were successful in putting them across?
- How has the event changed your relationship with the targets?
- How much time did you manage to spend talking seriously to each target individual?
- What concrete steps forward have you taken? For example, are you now able to talk on first-name terms, do you have access to their direct telephone line for the first time, are you confident they will now remember your name when you next approach them?

- What do you understand their perceptions of the host company to have been before the event?
- How have you been able to influence those perceptions?
- What specific marketing messages did you manage to get across to the targets – for example, changes in price, new product launches, changes of personnel?
- How have your perceptions of the targets changed as a result of getting to know them better?
- What did you manage to learn about their needs that you didn't know before?
- How can you serve those needs better?
- What will your next contact be with each of the target individuals?

If you can answer a list of questions like this, you will also be able to prepare a report on the event and the campaign that it is a part of. A document like this could be very useful a few months later when someone asks you how you can now justify the money spent on the event. To give a convincing answer, however, you must have moved at least one stage further with your targets, making whatever follow-up calls and actions were shown to be necessary, and exploiting any opportunities that opened up on the day.

Although it may be true that the real value of the event will not be obvious for years, if at all, that sort of argument generally carries very little weight with the people who actually allocate budgets for future activities. If you want other people in your organisation to believe in the power of corporate entertainment, you must give them some concrete facts and figures to look at, as well as explaining the longer term and more intangible benefits.

Your Next Move

There is always an excuse for at least one call immediately after the event, asking if guests enjoyed themselves and if they got home safely. Good manners will ensure that guests take the call, but the caller must then be ready to take the relationship on to the next stage with a request for an appointment or even for an order, if that is the next goal.

Hopefully you will have at least one thing you can follow up with each of the guests. They may have expressed an interest in a new product, in which case you can send them a brochure or arrange for a sales call or demonstration. They may have expressed dissatisfaction with some aspect of your service, in which case you can look into it, and then contact them to let them know how you are going to rectify matters.

It is vital that you make some sort of contact within the following few weeks, otherwise the initial impact of the event, and any warmth the guest felt towards you for organising it, will have begun to dissipate.

If you had a photographer at the event, you can arrange for framed prints to be made up of each of the guests and send them with a covering letter, thanking people for attending. Some organisers also have video teams at events, in order to be able to send guests tapes of the proceedings. It is an expensive alternative and may well be less effective. Guests receiving a video tape might watch it once, just to see themselves on television, but it is very unlikely that they will ever bother to look at it again. A framed photograph, however, can easily be put on a desk or an office wall, and will then stay there as a permanent reminder of the event and of the hosts.

Keep the Momentum Going

'In many cases it is more profitable to hold a number of events each year instead of just one, in order to keep up a campaign of regular contact,' says David Tonnison. 'It doesn't mean that you have to spend more; it just means spending differently.'

Internal Follow-up

If corporate entertainment has been used as part of an in-house motivation campaign or training scheme, then follow-up activities are equally important. Any advantages that have been gained by giving the target employees an enjoyable time will be quickly forgotten when they get back to the day-to-day frustrations of their jobs – unless you keep reminding them.

A newsletter about the event, photographs and thank-you letters will all help to keep the memory alive. It is also important to get feedback from them – anonymously if necessary. Did they enjoy the event? Would they like to do it again? What did they not enjoy about it? Is there anything they would rather do next time? If they could have a dream come true, what would it be?

All the feedback will be useful, even if it is facetious, because it will give you an idea of the impression the event made. If it has been greeted with uniform cynicism, then it obviously can't have been planned and executed effectively because it hasn't achieved the desired goals.

Only by finding out what people think, and what they want for the future, can you hope to do better next time.

Public Relations Add-ons

A successful event can also be a useful opportunity for general public relations. Pictures of the managing director being beaten in a motor-bike race by the office tea lady make a good story for any in-house magazine, and might get into a trade paper as well.

'When Coca-Cola were opening a new factory, with a

senior politician doing the honours,' says Chas Wheeler, 'we constructed a reception area completely out of Coke cans. That got a lot of coverage in the trade press.'

Companies that do use corporate entertainment are sometimes shy of talking about it. They believe that people in the company who are not involved will not understand why their colleagues are seen sipping champagne at the races, or shooting clay pigeons with a client. It can smack of élitism (especially as élitism may be one of the hooks you use to tickle the targets' fancy).

One of the goals of the campaign should therefore be to explain clearly to everyone in the company what is going on and why it is happening. If an event is being organised simply as a management perk, then those who are excluded will be quite right to complain, but if there is a genuine marketing reason for it, then the whole company should know about it, understand the reasoning behind it and hear about the results.

The more people within the company who are involved in the planning of the event, and who read about it afterwards, the more likely you are to be able to achieve major goals, such as changing attitudes or improving customer care.

Maintaining a Personal Relationship

Once you have laid the foundations for a personal relationship with a guest, then that relationship should never be allowed to falter.

While no one wants to be pestered, everyone likes to think that they are remembered by people they have met, even if there is a commercial reason for the relationship. The worst thing you could do is allow the relationship to slip back to being impersonal.

If you have got to know a client on first-name terms at an event, for instance, it would then be a disaster for that client to receive an impersonal letter from someone else in your department addressed 'Dear Mr Smith' or, worse still, 'Dear

Sir'. If something like that happens, it will convey the message that either you were being completely insincere when you told your client that you would be looking after their interests personally, or your company is so inefficient that one person in your department has no idea what the others are up to.

When you start a corporate entertainment campaign, you must be sure that you can handle the workload that may follow. If you are not going to be able to provide your targets with the level of personal involvement you claim to be offering, then you are wasting your time and money in trying to establish the relationships in the first place.

'It is my experience,' says Eddie Hoare, 'that anyone who starts using corporate entertainment as a marketing tool always comes back for more.'

Chapter Summary

- Have the goals clear from the start, and committed to paper.
- Keep referring back to them throughout the project, particularly the day before the event.
- Try to find ways of measuring results.
- Don't confuse successful administration with successful marketing.
- Always follow up.
- Try to find some concrete, short-term gains, as well as long-term ones.
- Photographs are usually more effective than videos.
- Get feedback from employees.
- Look for public relations opportunities.
- Make sure everyone in the company knows why the event happened and understands its context within the overall marketing campaign.
- Make sure any personal relationships formed do not slip away.

Chapter 14

Bribery and Corruption

When can a gift be seen as a bribe? This question has perplexed people for centuries, and probably always will. The dividing line is completely subjective. Something that one person sees as perfectly normal business practice, another sees as flagrant attempts to corrupt.

The key factor in decisions about whether or not to invite someone to a corporate entertainment event is whether it is *appropriate*. Is it appropriate that a person of that level should be entertained in that fashion? And the answer can come only from your own experience of your industry, or that of your advisers, and from your ability to distinguish between good and bad taste.

'There has to be a reason for inviting someone to an event.' explains Jim Bignall. 'You can't, for instance, just invite someone to Paris for the weekend. You can, however, invite them to Paris to watch a famous horserace, and while they are there they can do all the other things that they would enjoy.'

There is no real logic involved here. It all comes down to what is socially acceptable. Some companies strictly forbid their employees to accept any kind of gift from suppliers, particularly in the retailing business where manufacturers are so desperate to get their products on to the right shelves and the decision-making power is in the hands of a few people. You need to be aware of what the rules are in the companies you are targeting, so that you do not cross their line of acceptable behaviour.

164

How Does It Look to the Outside World?

As well as choosing events that are suitable to the industries in which you and your targets are working, you also need to bear in mind the impression you will be making on other groups that are important to your business.

When British Satellite Broadcasting (BSB) collapsed, a lot of media attention was focused on the fact that the top management had flown around the world with targets, taking them to watch the launching of satellites and providing other entertainments. No doubt at the time of planning, the trips seemed like sensible marketing methods, particularly in a company that was used to taking risks in every other way (launching satellite television stations at the time was a licence to burn money); in retrospect, it looked like a foolish and wasteful squandering of money BSB did not have.

On the other hand. Allied Dunbar, a highly successful and aggressive financial services company, is well known for motivating its sales people with lavish entertainment, as well as high rates of commission. Because they are successful, anyone who is impressed by the company's ability to sell would applaud the methods used. Although I do not have access to the figures – and they probably don't exist in any concrete form – the impression given is that Allied Dunbar spends far more on corporate entertainment than BSB ever did, but because it is easy to explain why they do it, and to point to the results, they are applauded where BSB was ridiculed.

If your company gets into financial trouble, or needs to go to the financial community for more money, and they start asking questions about how you spend their money, you need to be able to explain very clearly why you do things in the way you do. If you are unable to do so in terms they can understand, you will appear irresponsible at best and dishonest at worst. The impression can easily be given

165

– particularly if your company has a high profile and is written about in the media – that you are living the high life at the expense of employees, shareholders and backers. The image of senior managers strolling around golf courses or playing at being landed gentry while everyone else in the company is struggling to survive is not an attractive one. An activity that might be applauded as evidence of marketing flair in a successful company can be seen as the direct opposite in a company that is not thriving, and this must be taken into account when plans are being laid.

By the same token, of course, lavish corporate entertainment events could be used to give targets confidence in a company's financial situation. People are often willing to believe that what they see on the surface is a true demonstration of what is going on behind the scenes. This is the very argument that company chairmen have been using for years to justify keeping their Rolls-Royces at times when workforces are being cut, or investing in major advertising campaigns when markets are stagnant or shrinking. If you use corporate entertainment in this way, however, you must be aware that you run the risk of having the whole thing blow up in your face. But then, risk-taking plays a positive part in any dynamic business plan, provided that the risk is a calculated one.

Take Advice but Keep Control

The more expert advice and help you seek, the better your chances of getting the balance right, but always maintain control yourself. You must at all times know what is being done in your name and why. While there are consultancies and package-suppliers emerging who are doing their best to improve and maintain the standards of the industry, the market is still young and immature. This means that mistakes are going to be made and companies are going to take bad decisions. The troubles that beset Keith Prowse, which is far and away the market leader in corporate hospitality packages in the UK – they nearly went bankrupt and had to be saved by another company in 1991 – show just how erratic business can be, and how easily public confidence can be lost.

There have been problems in the past with dishonest and inept agencies and consultancies, and the scope for trouble is always there. A parallel case might be the development of the travel industry, which used to be beset by disasters, with companies disappearing overnight and leaving customers stranded with worthless tickets in foreign destinations. While customers who buy from the major players in the travel market are now well protected by trade bodies and the law, there will always be cut-price merchants who sail closer to the wind than is safe, and who consequently sink every so often. It is impossible to make anything completely safe, but you can always take sensible precautions.

Chapter Summary

- Always do what is 'appropriate'.
- If in doubt, take professional advice.
- There must be a concrete reason and purpose for any invitation.
- Be aware of the rules in your target companies.
- Ask yourself how the event would appear to others if your company went bankrupt tomorrow.
- Always be able to explain clearly why you are doing what you are doing.

Conclusion

Corporate entertainment is all around us, although half the time we don't even give it a second thought. Companies are pouring money into the restaurants that provide business lunches and dinners and the hotels that cater for conferences and travelling business people. The concept is ingrained so deeply into the worlds of selling, public relations, sales promotion and customer service that it is virtually impossible to distinguish it from everyday routine.

If a company is able to distinguish it, however, and can learn to plan and control it in the same way as it plans and controls its purchasing of plant and raw material, or the requirement of its staff, it will be unleashing an enormous force.

A company that analyses all its personal relationships, both inside and outside the company, and looks at the most effective way of developing them in order to increase loyalty and improve service, can't fail to improve its performance in virtually every sphere of activity.

The first step, therefore, is to recognise that corporate entertainment exists as a potential force, and then to harness it to the marketing cause.

Index

Spectrum Communications,
120–21
Stoll Moss Theatres, 9
Superbowl, 106
Supersports, 9
Swan, Paul, 120–21, 153

Tonnison, David, 3, 10, 25, 39,
131, 145, 158, 161

Travel Organisation, 131
Treasure Hunt, 129

Webster, Sarah, 135, 140–4
Wentworth Golf Club, 120
Wheeler, Chas, 42, 44, 48, 60,
62–3, 74, 79–80, 82, 84, 93, 101,
150, 154–5, 162
Wimbledon, 7, 84, 101, 113